Divination
Dictionary

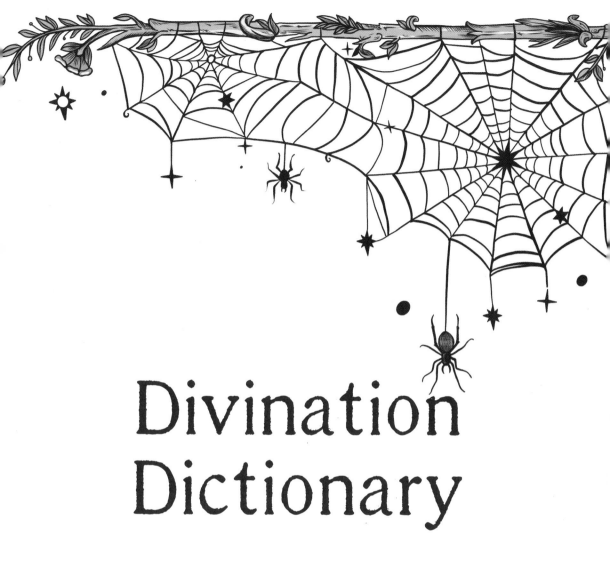

Divination
Dictionary

Lilian Verner-Bonds

Illustrations by
Coni Curi

STERLING ETHOS
New York

STERLING ETHOS
New York

ISBN 978-1-4549-4287-0

Distributed in Canada by
Sterling Publishing Co., Inc.,
c/o Canadian Manda Group,
664 Annette Street, Toronto,
Ontario M6S 2C8, Canada

For information about custom
editions, special sales, and premium
and corporate purchases, please contact
Sterling Special Sales at 800-805-5489
or specialsales@sterlingpublishing.com.

Manufactured in Singapore

10 9 8 7 6 5 4 3 2 1

sterlingpublishing.com

QUAR.337795

Senior Art Editor: Martina Calvio
Designer: Karin Skånberg
Illustrator: Coni Curi
Editor: Claire Waite Brown
Publisher: Samantha Warrington

Contents

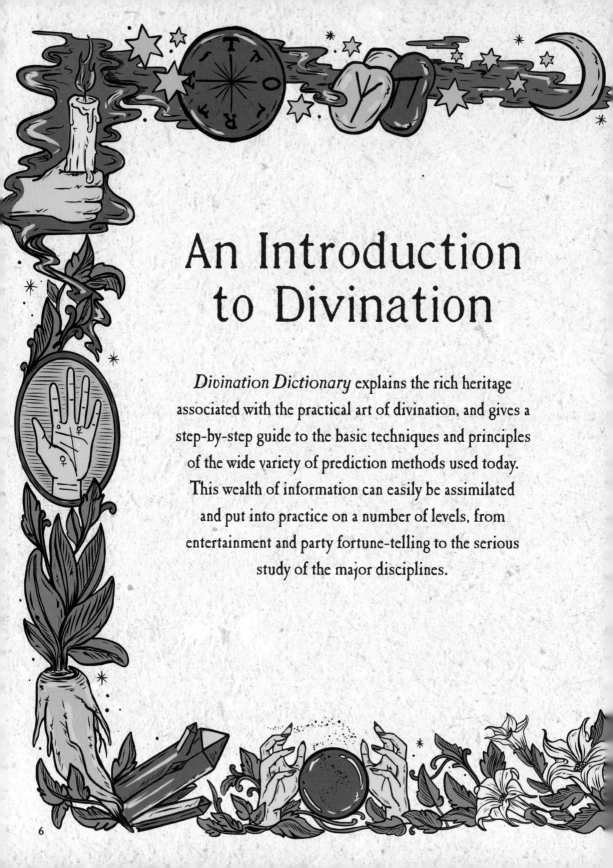

An Introduction to Divination

Divination Dictionary explains the rich heritage associated with the practical art of divination, and gives a step-by-step guide to the basic techniques and principles of the wide variety of prediction methods used today. This wealth of information can easily be assimilated and put into practice on a number of levels, from entertainment and party fortune-telling to the serious study of the major disciplines.

The goal of this book is to enable you to interpret your own and your friends' future—and to answer those questions that provide positive and fruitful planning to make the best of the years ahead.

In divination, anything you care to use can foretell, whether it be cards, pebbles, animals, twigs, dice, or a host of other things. The patterns and shapes of nature and objects give the diviner hints at truth when the intuition is really operating. Every object and tool speaks in its own special language. You are encouraged to try working with as many prediction methods as possible to find the ones with which you most resonate. This will enable you to tap into all the majestic power of the universe.

Authorities are increasingly recognizing that psychic ability is a widespread human potential, placing it in the same mental arena as intuition, and suggest that everyone has it to some extent. Even if it is lying latent and undiscovered, this talent can be activated. The Seer's Apprenticeship section (see pages 10–13) provides a process for developing clairvoyant skills on an individual basis. Intuition is a form of knowledge that hides the means by which it is accomplished. This book fills in the missing pieces of the jigsaw to reveal the secret knowledge underlying the principles of fortune-telling.

The book is divided into five chapters. Instructions are given for the use and interpretation of various methods of divination using the techniques and objects listed in each chapter.

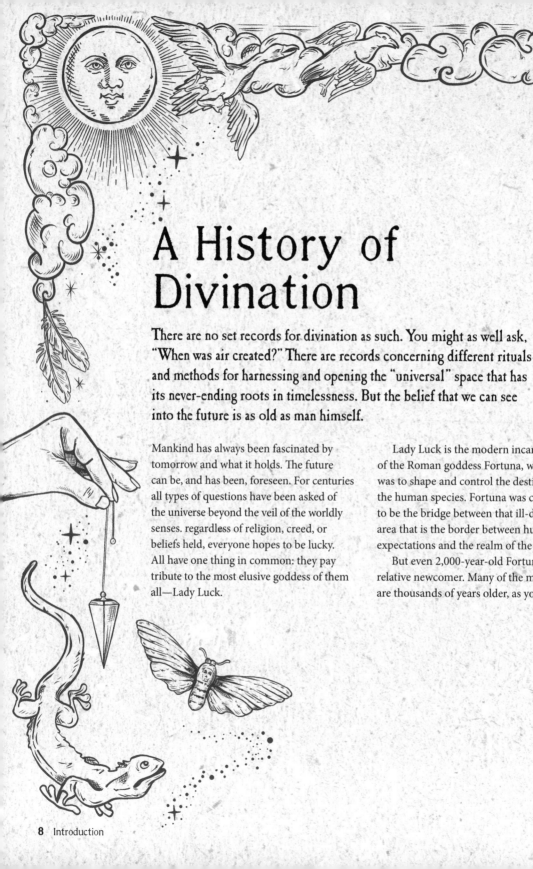

A History of Divination

There are no set records for divination as such. You might as well ask, "When was air created?" There are records concerning different rituals and methods for harnessing and opening the "universal" space that has its never-ending roots in timelessness. But the belief that we can see into the future is as old as man himself.

Mankind has always been fascinated by tomorrow and what it holds. The future can be, and has been, foreseen. For centuries all types of questions have been asked of the universe beyond the veil of the worldly senses. regardless of religion, creed, or beliefs held, everyone hopes to be lucky. All have one thing in common: they pay tribute to the most elusive goddess of them all—Lady Luck.

Lady Luck is the modern incarnation of the Roman goddess Fortuna, whose role was to shape and control the destinies of the human species. Fortuna was considered to be the bridge between that ill-defined area that is the border between human expectations and the realm of the gods.

But even 2,000-year-old Fortuna is a relative newcomer. Many of the methods are thousands of years older, as you will discover in the introductions to each means of divination presented here. Each country or culture throughout history has, through the centuries, had its own understanding of fortune's revelations, and the methods that can be used to help make decisions in life. Many of the present-day means of fortune-telling were brought to the West and popularized by the Romany people, although others, such as astrology, have been with us since records began.

Man has always been intuitively aware of what is a good sign—and what is not. Much of this intuitive or psychic sense became submerged when the "scientific" world began. But, whether it be a rebellion against the industrial and scientific age when it seemed that machines took over man's senses and sensibilities, or a reawakening of ancient, inner echoes, there has been a renewed interest in and revival of the prophetic arts.

In recent times, research has gone into clairvoyance, telepathy, and precognition, indicating that extrasensory powers or the occurrence of phenomena—working apparently independently of the known physical laws—may not just be the prerogative of a gifted few. They are, after all, common to all mankind. Each and every one of us can reach into that state of divine space and extract the insights that are commonly called "fortune-telling."

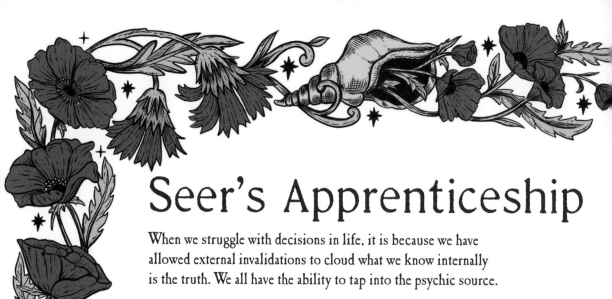

Seer's Apprenticeship

When we struggle with decisions in life, it is because we have allowed external invalidations to cloud what we know internally is the truth. We all have the ability to tap into the psychic source.

This psychic source can bring greater understanding of life. It isn't by chance that you are reading this now—it's called synchronicity, which means you are ready and have been called. If you have the courage to listen to the voice that has no sound, the veil of secrecy will begin to lift from your inner vision, revealing to you prospects for health, harmony, and abundance.

Harmonizing—the internal switch-on

To gain access to predictive realms, you must first connect to your intuition. Then you can find the internal mechanism that enables you to make correct choices in your life. All that is required for "spirit" to come through is for you to be available. You cannot be engaged elsewhere while tuning in. Quick flashes can appear momentarily, but for more substantial understanding you will have to focus on the "internal self."

Self-harmony exercise
This simple three-breath harmonizer will help you focus on the inner self, preparing you to open up your psychic channel to receive from the infinite.

1. Sit quietly with your back against a chair so that your spine is straight. Knees, legs and ankles must be uncrossed, with your feet flat on the floor. Hands are unclasped, and resting comfortably by your side or on your thighs. This relaxed state enables energy within your body to flow freely.

2. Take a large breath in through your nose and hold it for as long as you can, counting slowly. The aim is to be able to hold your breath for 35 counts. You may not be able to do this at first but that does not matter. In time you will improve. Whatever you do, do not hold for longer than you feel it is safe to do so. You can work your way up to the magic 35 counts gradually over several sessions, if necessary.

3. Repeat the breath hold twice more. At first you may experience dizziness or a surge of energy, which is perfectly normal.

Tuning into your psychic ability

Once you've harmonized yourself, your aim is to enter into the space called the universal realm of intelligence, from which all knowledge springs. It is a good idea to begin to develop clairvoyance. The clairvoyant who sees visions, the clairaudient who hears messages, the psychic, medium, seer, prophet, oracle, or Tarot card reader—they all come within the fortune-telling realm. The only difference between them is their technique. They all tune into the same source to connect into their psychic ability for divination. There will be a method that is appropriate for you to pick up energy that is the inner language of heaven.

Meditation: unity process
Meditation can help you to access your psychic ability.

1. Lie down on a floor or bed so that you are relaxed. Concentrate on breathing deeply and easily.

2. Close your eyes and visualize above your body the screen of a TV set. Switch it on and observe what appears on the screen—what is being played or acted out. It could be showing ordinary everyday activities, a simple object, symbol, or maybe a color. You may get just a feeling or a sense.

3. Remain in this state for seven minutes. Mentally turn off the screen and focus on your breath, letting it return to its own natural rhythm.

4. Open your eyes when you feel ready. It is important to remember what you have experienced and write it down immediately. Ask yourself: Did I feel happy or sad? What does what I saw mean? Give yourself quiet time to decipher and understand what was being shown to you.

5. Congratulations! Your psychic ability has just begun to kick in!

Nature's forces

Harnessing the forces of nature as a guide and adviser is so easy and natural, as you will discover in the Fortunes from Nature chapter of the book (see page 36). All the elements—earth, air, fire, and water—have had an important part to play in the divinatory arts. Beginning 24 hours before working with nature's forces, start deacidifying the body by eating no meat or dairy products, and cleanse the system with any green vegetable soup. Eat only fruit, with the exception of grapefruit, oranges, and plums. Drink only water. Please note that this regimen should be cleared with your doctor.

Tools for instant fortune-telling

Fortune-telling tools—such as cards, the palm of the inquirer (or the "Querant"), fire, and crystal balls—are used as connectors, leads into the seer's realm. They are keys that unlock your psyche and launch you off! Every object and tool used speaks in its own special language, giving instant clues and insights. But always bear in mind the following when using your chosen tools.

• To prepare your hands to use tools, make a cleanser with salt moistened with only clear, warm water. Rub your hands with it and rinse.

• Do not allow anyone else to use or work with your personal equipment.

• When they are not in use, always wrap tools in a piece of black or purple silk, and put them in a safe place away from direct sunlight to protect them.

• At the end of the day, take a cleansing bath in which sea salt has been placed in order to release toxins from the skin.

Seer's toolbox
Let the information and exercises in this book help you to build your own seer's toolbox.

Amulets
Nature; protection; and good fortune

The word amulet has its origins in the Latin word *amuletum*, meaning a "thing," be it bracelet, trinket, metal, or parchment, inscribed with magical signs. Amulets are worn or carried as charms, possessing energy to bring fortune to the wearer because of the quality of their features.

Nature amulets
The sacred horse and the poppy

A talisman is an object over which a rite has been completed to imbue it with a specific intention. It has the task of warding off ill luck as well as supporting and giving energy to the special purpose for which it has been chosen.

Vegetable and animal symbols have a high place in the list of amulets, the belief being that favorable influences of luck and protection are inherent in nature's objects. The horse became a sacred symbol of nature early on. Stone horses guarded the imperial tombs of Nanking, and the prehistoric White Horse cut into a hillside in England is thought to be a representation of the Celtic horse goddess Epona, "the Divine Horse."

The poppy flower depicts Mother Nature, embracing the rise of the moon, fertility, and abundance. Divination emerges from the flower's symbolism, the five-fold petals representing the human senses, the light of the sun, and the primeval water. The cup of the flower is a perfect manifestation of the wheel of fortune: the poppy is a bringer both of beauty and of dissipation through its opium, revealing both the good and bad omens of nature.

Make your own
To make and energize your own nature amulets, see page 19.

Protection amulet
Thor's hammer

Amulets can emit protective powers to ward off evil and attract favorable influences. Thor's famous double-sided hammer, enabling it to strike true with each throw, represents the thunder god's masculine energy—the avenging power that upholds justice. This force offers protection and crushes before it all darkness and evil.

Thor—said to be the eldest son of Odin—was the hero of warriors, striding through the sky brandishing his magical hammer (called *Mjollnir*) defending both gods and humans from the threat of invaders. Thor's name survives in the word Thursday, meaning Thor's day.

A hammer may be considered an object of brute force, but, when associated with Thor, it becomes a celestial instrument because of its association with spiritual willpower—shattering enslavement and bringing freedom. The hammer then becomes an implement of magical protection.

The action of this amulet is to bring Thor's great protection to the owner—protection against adversity and the source of ill omens—and to give safety and strength while traveling along the path of existence.

Make your own
It is a good idea to perform a protection ritual before working with any divination techniques, so to make and energize your own protection amulet, see page 19.

Good fortune amulet
The sacred Egyptian scarab beetle

The Egyptian scarab beetle is known as the greatest amulet ever, revered because of its spirit-of-life connection. It was depicted in ancient Egypt as the dung beetle, carrying between its two front legs a huge solar ball.

An actual dung beetle rolls its ball of dung from east to west following the direction of the sun. Eventually, its ball is rolled into a hole in the earth. The beetle goes into hiding in the dark hole for 28 days, emerging on the 29th day to throw the ball into water, where the baby scarabs emerge. It was believed that, since the sun rolls its ball daily across the sky, that the sun must be the original scarab. The ball of dung became symbolized as possessing the internal spirit of new birth, the embryo of immortality, and the celestial heart.

The scarab not only represented the path of the sun and self-creative power, but also invoked renewal, resurrection, immortality, and divine wisdom. It held the key of life, integrating both male and female fertility for the future, and directing and regulating the continual productive powers of nature. It represented both death and life, with the promise of dawn and a new tomorrow. Jars containing scarab beetles have been found in graves dating back from before 3500 BC.

Scarabs have been fashioned out of various metals and can be found on Tutankhamen's coffin, with outspread wings evoking the gods.

Make your own
To make and energize your own good fortune amulet, see page 19.

Nature amulet

Nature amulet

Protection amulet

Good fortune amulet

Amulets
Cut out and keep

Nature amulet

Nature amulet

Good fortune amulet

Protection amulet

Nature amulets

The combination of the protective white horse and poppy encompasses positive earthly spirits, and protects from any evil entities through the Divine Horse.

1. Cut out the horse and poppy images opposite—alternatively you can color photocopy them or trace and color them yourself.

2. To energize your amulets, visualize a wand of transparent ethereal matter held between the curved forefinger and thumb of your left hand—a stick of bright strong light vibrating at an intense rate.

3. Wave it over your amulet backward and forward three times. The "light" wash will awaken and strengthen your amulet's energy and help your nature amulet give added protection.

4. To carry this nature amulet with you, fold the images up and put them in a sealed white envelope.

Protection amulet

The hammer-source of Thor will keep vigil and be on guard, keeping you safe and secure as you venture into the world of fortune-telling.

1. Cut out the hammer image opposite—alternatively you can color photocopy it or trace and color it yourself.

2. To energize the amulet, place the center of your palm down onto Thor's hammer and hold it there for 21 seconds.

3. Allow the energy of the hammer to travel through your palm and into your bloodstream. Your circulation will engulf your body with a protective vibration.

Good fortune amulet

Chapter 30 of the Book of the Dead requires that a Royal Scarab have the pharaoh's name inscribed on its belly so that it will not witness against him at the day of judgment. You can use a similar process to energize your scarab amulet.

1. Cut out the scarab image opposite—alternatively you can color photocopy it or trace and color it yourself.

2. To transform the amulet into a personalized talisman and good luck charm, write your signature across the underside of the beetle. Your signature will seal the scarab's power to work only for you.

Chapter 1
Revelations Within Us

Our minds and bodies carry the imprint of our fates. This ancient belief is now experiencing a rebirth. By reading those signs and indications, we gain access to the patterns of our lives, upon which all fortune is built. We now understand that we need to work from the inside out, rather than always seeking external signs. Our palms, our faces, our dreams, all have been shaped by our own individual essence. But the rational person might ask: "Why should they be?"

Much of the work of psychics and mediums has been dismissed because of a lack of understanding of what takes place. Throughout history they have spontaneously offered answers without being able to say how. Carl Jung, one of the most respected psychologists of the twentieth century, highlighted the actual inner process. Jung was a great believer in divination, and, when treating a patient, always had a birth horoscope cast to determine what shaping influences were present at the start of the person's life. He didn't believe that the influences caused the events of that life, but rather that they were, in his term, "meaningful coincidences." In other words, "anything that happens at a particular moment of time has the qualities of that moment of time." So it is within ourselves: We all carry internally the imprint of the time and place we came into the world—a time and place that reflects our individual fates. We can, as "recording machines," tap into our past, present, and future.

In the end, there cannot be any connection to the outside—to the infinite—if we do not connect to our personal inner self. The tools and techniques of divination may be considered that which propels us in our connection, but it does that only if our internal switch has been turned on to the cosmic flow. In this section you will discover a number of tried and trusted ways of discovering fate and fortune from the imprint within yourself.

Palmistry

The future in your hand

The Romanies could tell your fortune by your hand shape alone. Apart from the obvious feel of rough skin that told them you were a laborer, or the soft skin that hinted at a lady, the shape of the palm and fingertips gave the palm reader insight—favorable or unfavorable—into the inquirer's future.

The benefit of "far-seeing" through palmistry is that steps can be taken to correct any adversities that may be indicated. This means that we do not have to remain victims to the future! In this section you can discover for yourself the hand shapes that reflect the underlying currents of fate and fortune—good luck or bad luck—and, armed with this knowledge take control of your future.

The dominant hand

Which hand do you read from? The hand of your future fortunes is your dominant hand, called in palmistry the "active" hand: If you are right-handed, it is your right hand; if left-handed, your left.

The square hand
Down to earth

The square hand literally has square fingertips and a square look about it, usually on a short, fairly squat palm. The characteristics are practicality and conventionality. It is a useful hand—those with square hands can turn those hands to anything. They are the salt of the earth. Industry, business, and commerce are suited to them because they have methodical minds and adhere to the rules.

Fortunate This particular shape of hand is the most materialistically lucky. With these hands your dreams come true because they have the Midas touch in business, and they usually have exceptionally good fortune in making deals.

Unfortunate People with these hands need to listen to their hearts as well as their heads. Rigidity and dogmatism can prevent them grasping at opportunities.

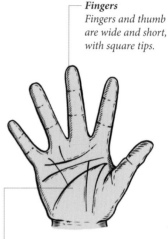

Fingers
Fingers and thumb are wide and short, with square tips.

Palm
The palm of the square hand appears short and broad.

The conic hand
Creative and artistic

The conic hand is an artistic hand. The palm will be longer and more slender than that of the square hand, and the fingertips will be rounded. There is a restlessness about the personality, forever seeking stimulating challenges, but there is quite often a problematical love life. People with these hands never stand still long enough to gather any roots. Personal comforts are a priority, but these people can also be generous, even overly so. Those with conic hands are extremely creative and love the arts. They would rather work for the love of it than for money.

Fortunate This hand is considered reasonably lucky. There is a balance of good fortune.

Unfortunate If their tendencies to overgenerosity and getting carried away by their flair come to the fore, they squander what they have gained. A case of "easy come, easy go."

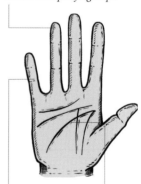

Fingertips
The conic hand has rounded or almond-shaped fingertips.

Fingers
The long and slim fingers of the conic hand denote creativity.

Palm
A long, slender palm is typical of the conic hand.

The spatulate hand
Action and inventiveness

The shape of a spatulate hand can be recognized by the spreading out of the ends of the fingertips like a fan. The rest of the hand may be a mixture of the square and conic shapes. People with these hands are extremely unconventional in their thinking and ways of behavior, and very quick-witted and fast to act. They can be great fun to be around since they are stimulating, self-confident, and resourceful. Original and with an independent spirit, they do not take kindly to a mundane nine-to-five job.

Fortunate This particular shape will draw to it either great fortune or nothing at all.

Unfortunate They are prone to having pie-in-the-sky ideas that other people tend to steal, resulting in a failure to profit from their own endeavors. Grass doesn't grow under their feet, which can make them difficult to keep up with.

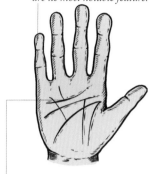

Fingertips
The distinctive splayed fingertips of the spatulate hand are its most notable feature.

Palm
The spatulate hand can have a mixture of square and conic hand characteristics.

The psychic hand
Imaginative and the medium

The psychic hand is said to be the most beautiful hand shape of all. The fingertips are long and pointed, tapering to almost nothing. The rest of the hand is small and slender and extremely delicate. It is called a psychic hand because the tips of the fingers are able to receive energy impulses from the atmosphere. Rather inclined to idealism, people with these hands have difficulty surviving in the real world, because they are not programmed to deal with the nitty-gritty. They have a need to be looked after, because they can be easily duped through being too trustful. It is hard to judge them by ordinary standards.

Fortunate The truly gifted psychic is indicated by the shape of this hand. They are imbued with insights and intuitive knowledge.

Unfortunate This is not considered to be the luckiest of hands. They are unable to draw to themselves that pot of gold on Earth that is desired unless they are fortunate enough to meet someone else who supplies their needs. Then, it is luck indeed!

Fingers
Long fingers that are slim and delicate in appearance are typical of the psychic hand.

Fingertips
On the psychic hand the tips of the fingers are pointed.

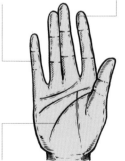

Palm
The psychic hand looks slight and small and has a narrow palm.

The philosophical hand
Studious and level-headed

The philosophical hand is easily recognized by its long, angular shape with bony fingers. The fingertips are usually long and round with a slight saucer shape. The main characteristic of this shape of hand is the knotted, large knuckles and finger joints. Possessing this type of hand means there is a great understanding of the world's workings inside and out. These people are great humanists, and individualism is their key. They have extreme patience and great tenacity to follow through on anything they have started. As far as success is concerned, they have a natural wisdom that unfortunately rarely leads to gold.

Fortunate People with this hand shape have the ability to follow through to the end regardless. Patience is rewarded. Biding one's time long enough eventually brings good luck and fortune.

Unfortunate They do not look before they leap, and tend to be unlucky when they act before they have thought things through.

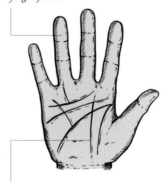

Fingers
The most noticeable feature of the philosophical hand is the prominent finger joints.

Palm
The palm of this hand tends to be long and angular.

The mixed hand
All sorts

To recognize the mixed-shape hand look to the fingers. The fingertips will have a mixture of all or some of the other shapes. The palm could be any shape—square, round, long, or short; but the mixed-shape fingertips govern its character. Great adaptability is always present. These people have the ability to bring to the fore any action that is required, because they have access to various sources of information at their fingertips. Extremely eloquent in speech, they make good diplomats. They have an uncanny ability to anticipate happenings and outcomes, which puts them in the position of always being one step ahead.

Fortunate A lucky mixture here, which means that they always have hope that tomorrow brings a better day, and the good luck that they are seeking—which it usually does. If they lose a dollar today, they will find $20 tomorrow! They are natural-born lottery winners.

Unfortunate On the downside, they can be scatterbrained and become addictive gamblers.

Mixed tips
The ring finger has a square tip, while the index and little fingers are rounded.

Palm
The mixed hand palm might be slim at the top and wide and square at the bottom.

Reading hand lines

The major hand lines are shown below. The heart, head, and life lines appear on most palms but not everyone has clearly marked mercury, fate, or sun lines. Regard each line as a map guiding you along its path, giving information along the way.

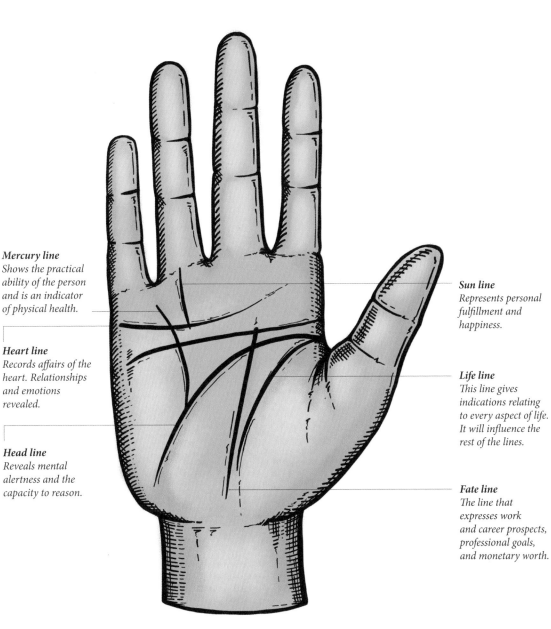

Mercury line
Shows the practical ability of the person and is an indicator of physical health.

Heart line
Records affairs of the heart. Relationships and emotions revealed.

Head line
Reveals mental alertness and the capacity to reason.

Sun line
Represents personal fulfillment and happiness.

Life line
This line gives indications relating to every aspect of life. It will influence the rest of the lines.

Fate line
The line that expresses work and career prospects, professional goals, and monetary worth.

Physiognomy
Insights from the mirror of the soul

Physiognomy is the art of analysis from the physical features of the face. The face is regarded as the mirror of the soul. Physiognomy is recorded as early as 1800 B.C. and was practiced by the philosophers Socrates, Hippocrates, and, later, Aristotle as a means of forecasting good or evil.

Physiognomy was never an organized movement or taken seriously until Johann Kaspar Lavater wrote a book about it and made it popular in the nineteenth century. He was followed by Mary Olmstead Stanton. Her methods were published in 1890, giving a vast and precise guideline that is still followed today.

The influence on the brain

Stanton believed that the organs of the body, such as the kidneys, lungs, liver, and heart, had an influence on the brain. This registered in a person's consciousness, integrity, and morality, and was in turn represented in the face. The twentieth century has seen a serious revival in understanding the facial motif and how it reflects the vital functioning of the internal organs.

Facial-feature fortunes

The face, thought to reflect the inner soul and nature of the person, is used by the fortune-teller as a sure means of assessing whether a lucky or unlucky life lies ahead. Most faces will have a combination of lucky and unlucky features, so if falls upon the reader to decide which side the balance of fate falls upon.

Nose

Big Great physical energy, zest, and drive; brings good fortune.

Small Hard to make a living; nothing comes easily; bad luck.

Nostrils

Large The wheeler-dealer and lucky.
Small Lonely and unlucky.

Eyelashes

Long Generous and lucky.
Short or sparse Draws misfortune.

Eyes

Large Show a happy person who is ready for success; fortunate sign.

Small: Narrow and mean-spirited; a suspicious nature; unfortunate luck.

Mouth

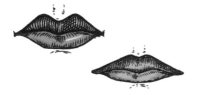

Large A large mouth with full lips shows a generous disposition, encouraging a full and bountiful life; good luck.

Small Indicates a difficult life, always held back—particularly if the lips are thin; elusive luck.

Ears

 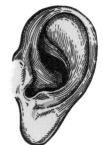

Big Indicate abundance, particularly with large lobes; a sexual nature; great self-confidence; extremely lucky.

Small Inclined to a lack of character; always short-changed; unlucky.

Cephalomancy

Reading from the skull

Well into the seventeenth century, the skull was valued in many societies as the seat of a person's soul and was associated with death. The inside of the bones were considered the center of psychic energy. In other words, the root of life existed in the skull.

Alchemists believed the skull was a receptacle of transmutation, able to act as a psychic charge. Skulls played a considerable part in medicine and magic, and mixtures of herbs were placed into the skull and used for healing purposes.

The skull's messages

Originally, readings for good or ill omens were taken from the skulls of animals, such as goats, horses, or bullocks. The human skull was also believed to contain supernatural qualities. It was said that if you asked a question of a skull, you would receive your answer. The spirit of the skull hints to all to drink deeply of life, and if we peer into the eyeless sockets we may find and read fate's messages while our unconsciousness is in contact with the unknown.

Divining from the skull

Although it's not easy to come by a genuine skull of any kind, you can usually get a plastic or ceramic one from a novelty or artifact shop. You need a hollow skull, so that a piece of paper inserted into an eye socket will fall through to the table underneath.

Spiritual home
The skull was worshipped by ancient cultures as the home of the spirit.

1. Place the hollow skull on a wooden or glass surface. In black ink write your question on a piece of white paper.

2. On an equal-sized piece of red paper, write the word "yes" in black ink.

3. On an equal-sized piece of blue paper, write the word "no," also in black ink.

4. Fold all three up equally.

5. Place the question paper inside the skull.

6. Place the red "yes" through the skull's right eye socket, and the blue "no" through the left.

7. Place a white cloth over the skull, and, keeping your eyes closed, remove the skull from the table.

8. With your eyes still closed, swirl the three pieces of paper around on the table.

9. Allow your fingers to retrieve two pieces of paper. The one remaining is your answer. If that piece is the question paper, it means that fate is not yet willing to reveal your fortune to you.

Oneiromancy
Fortune-telling through dreams

Telling the future through dreams was regarded as an established science in ancient times. An early Egyptian papyrus has been found, recording over 200 dreams and their meanings. Medieval artists often depicted the Old Testament dream of the Egyptian Pharaoh as interpreted by Joseph, who correctly predicted seven years of plenty followed by seven years of famine.

An age-old belief is that dreams are part of an existence mysteriously different from our everyday life—ventures into an enigmatic otherworld. We can learn about important events when we understand the visions we receive in our dreams.

Freud, Jung, and the world of dreams

The interpretation of dreams lost its high profile and respected position through the ages, becoming the domain of gypsies, or reduced to party games and trickery. In the twentieth century it took two eminent psychoanalysts, Freud and then Jung, to make dream analysis respectable again. Freud reported dreams as an outworking of our subconscious mind and desires, whereas Jung associated dreams with less worldly aspirations.

Dream diary

When wishing to analyze your dreams write each one down immediately upon waking. This way you will be able to recall most of it, whereas if you leave it until later some of its significance and details may be forgotten. Some guidance for interpreting dreams is offered on pages 30–31. Keeping a record of your dreams allows you to check whether there is a recurring situation, or whether any patterns are revealed.

You might also wish to sleep with a dream catcher hanging above your bed. This Native American device is believed to ensnare bad dreams before they get to you, while letting positive dreams through.

Dream catcher
The gossamer threads woven into a dream catcher are believed to block bad dreams.

Dream interpretation

Many of the scenes that we experience while dreaming can be grouped into basic themes. Look out for these themes to get an understanding of the direction and insights of the dream.

Colors

Strong colors in your dreams, such as bright red, orange, and yellow, bestow energy and action for the future, and are good luck. Green pinpoints money issues and relationships; if the green is dark it is not a good omen for these areas. Blue, indigo, and purple suggest it is time to rethink and bide your time within whatever dream scene you are viewing. A dream that is black and white suggests it's from the past; a dream full of color is a prediction for the future.

House

This represents the self. The bedroom represents your sexual nature, the kitchen your working life, and the basement your subconscious.

Earth

Any dream connected to the earth is a good omen and suggests rich future possibilities.

Dark heavy earth is a warning to break away from tradition and be careful not to get stuck in a rut in the future.

Time

Many dreams involve a time sense. Look carefully to see what this sense is telling you. For example, a clock indicates that time is of the essence and you had better get a move on.

Body

Hands and arms are linked to your creativity; mouth and teeth to the unspoken word; and your hair means you'd better start to think clearly before you act if you are to have good luck.

Action

Any dream that depicts action, such as working or running, indicates career prospects. Running might suggest that an escape from a situation is necessary. Dreaming of work can predict a change of career direction.

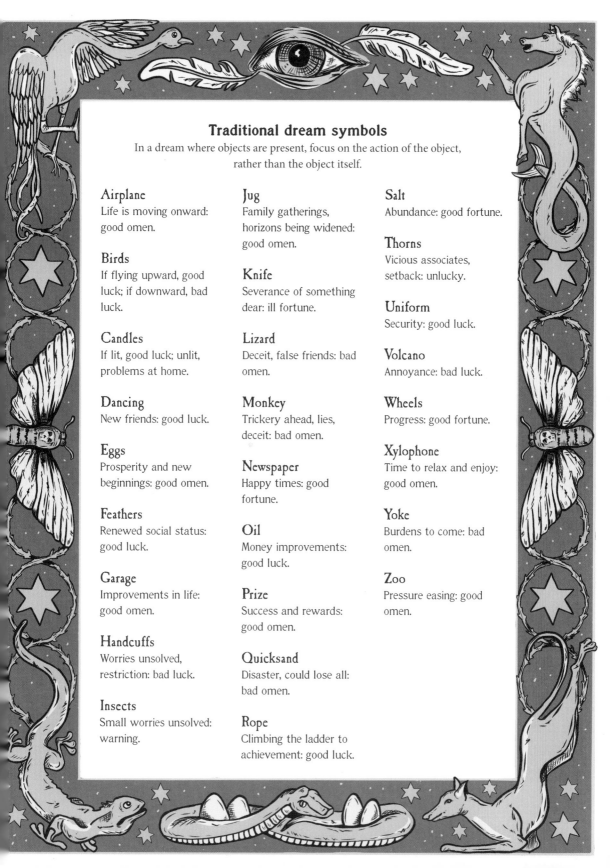

Traditional dream symbols

In a dream where objects are present, focus on the action of the object, rather than the object itself.

Airplane
Life is moving onward: good omen.

Birds
If flying upward, good luck; if downward, bad luck.

Candles
If lit, good luck; unlit, problems at home.

Dancing
New friends: good luck.

Eggs
Prosperity and new beginnings: good omen.

Feathers
Renewed social status: good luck.

Garage
Improvements in life: good omen.

Handcuffs
Worries unsolved, restriction: bad luck.

Insects
Small worries unsolved: warning.

Jug
Family gatherings, horizons being widened: good omen.

Knife
Severance of something dear: ill fortune.

Lizard
Deceit, false friends: bad omen.

Monkey
Trickery ahead, lies, deceit: bad omen.

Newspaper
Happy times: good fortune.

Oil
Money improvements: good luck.

Prize
Success and rewards: good omen.

Quicksand
Disaster, could lose all: bad omen.

Rope
Climbing the ladder to achievement: good luck.

Salt
Abundance: good fortune.

Thorns
Vicious associates, setback: unlucky.

Uniform
Security: good luck.

Volcano
Annoyance: bad luck.

Wheels
Progress: good fortune.

Xylophone
Time to relax and enjoy: good omen.

Yoke
Burdens to come: bad omen.

Zoo
Pressure easing: good omen.

Graphology

Handwriting analysis

Handwriting analysis—graphology—is a very old science. Thousands of years ago the Chinese used it to analyze their calligraphy. The Romans used graphology extensively, and it saw a renewal in the Middle Ages among the few literate people of the day. In modern times psychologists, beginning with Carl Jung, have come to recognize it as a valid indicator of character and personality.

The most common use of graphology is in character analysis, however it is also used to assess the fortune of the writer, since, to a large degree character and fortune go hand in hand.

The major indicators that are easily evaluated are zones and letters. Start with the zones.

The zones

Imagine letters divided into three sections: the main body of the letters is the middle zone, the descenders are the lower zone, and the ascenders are the upper zone. Fortune is indicated from the zones as follows:

• If the letters of the middle zone are larger than those of the upper and lower zones, there is a strength and practicality that will bring good fortune in worldly affairs. The spiritual life may suffer, however, and there can be a tendency to ignore the needs of the body, meaning that fortunes may not be as rosy in these areas.

• If the upper zone is the largest, there may be a tendency to ignore the practical realities of life, and fortune will pass by.

• Large loops in the lower zone show a self-centeredness that may bring good fortune in some areas, but can also drive people away. Loops coming straight down are propitious: they indicate an ability to focus and create one's own good fortune.

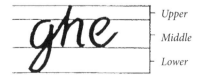

Upper
Middle
Lower

The letters

After assessing the zones, look at individual letters. There are some letters in particular that are highly indicative of both character traits and fortune.

Capital "M"	Capital "I"	Lowercase "t"	Lowercase "i"	Lowercase "a" and "o"
A high first stroke indicates that the writer has a healthy ego and a tendency to attract good fortune.	A capital "I" larger than other capital letters shows vanity and self absorption. Willfulness brings fortune, but at the expense of fortune in others.	A crossbar above or just on the stem shows a daydreamer if light, or a strong imagination if heavy.	An elongated dot shows a person of great critical sensitivity. Intuitive decisions prove lucky.	A small, open "a" or "o" reflects a person who is talkative to the point of being a gossip. Envy of other people's good fortune means they are unable to appreciate their own.
If the first stroke is lower, fortunes may be less kind—you may be buffeted by the opinions of others.	A capital "I" that is much smaller than the other capitals shows timidity and a weakness of personality. The writer may struggle to find good fortune anywhere.	A long bar extended over the entire word is a sign of ambition. The writer will grasp good fortune.	Thick and heavy dots reveal a bad temper and even brutality. Good fortune is driven away.	
If the "M" is rounded, there is likely to be a lack of forcefulness in the personality; luck not seized will pass by.	An inflated capital "I" shows an exaggerated self-importance. As before, willfulness may force good fortune in some areas, but at the expense of other people.	Timidity and a lack of self-assurance is revealed by a short bar. The writer may be afraid to take chances.	A dot forming a small arc shows great powers of observation. The writer makes their own luck.	When these letters are closed or knotted, a very self-contained and discreet person is shown. After hard work and great efforts the writer will find good fortune.
If the "M" is very angular, the writer demonstrates drive and forcefulness, which creates its own luck.	A capital "I" that has breaks in it shows a disconnection of the personality. The writer has a tendency to overlook good fortune when it appears.	A strong bar crossing well to the right is an indicator of self-confidence. This person attracts luck in life.		

Psychic Drawing
Guidance from the spirits

Psychic drawing or writing is considered to be dictation from a deceased spirit, giving guidance to the living with messages that are channeled through the sitter and onto paper. This form of psychic drawing is, in effect, a conscious dream.

Psychic drawing was first reported in the 1840s from the Mesmerists Movement, where channeled talking and writing were practiced while in a hypnotic trance. The messages were interpreted as information coming through spirit guides from those who had passed on. It became popular in the United States and quickly spread to the rest of the West. David Duguld from Scotland in 1870 and Marion Gruzewski of Poland during the 1920s expanded psychic drawing into a "painting-in-the-dark" experience.

Reading the images
Any form of intuitive ability can be accessed by the technique of psychic drawing. With perception, all markings that appear on the paper can lead to fortune-telling revelations.

Picture this
Almost anyone can produce, by means of automatic writing or painting, information that can be assessed for fortune-telling. The Automist—as the reader is called—will bring about a relaxed state of mind similar to a trance, and may not recall anything at all afterward. The pictures you receive in the early stages may be very crude, with just a letter or a figure appearing on the page. Keep trying, and with perseverance and practice some spiritual and practical insights can be gained. Whether it is spirit, telepathy, or psychic ability that is guiding the hand of the writer or painter, it can be used to seek fortune and enlightenment.

1. To prepare yourself to practice this mystical experience, sit quietly in a peaceful place holding a pen, colored pencil, or a paintbrush with a palette of paints, over a piece of paper. You may find that you want to close your eyes or your mind to your immediate surroundings.

2. Become conscious of your arm. Let it disassociate itself from the rest of your body and move at random. Let your hand be guided over the paper.

3. Automatic scripts flow from spirit, in harmony with cosmic law. Study, meditate, and eventually you will be able to decipher the signs for good or ill omens that have been sent to you from the gods of fortune.

Chapter 2

Fortunes From Nature

Your body vibrates at a high, powerful rate. Each of us is a miniature universe
that resonates with everything about us. We are all in direct contact with nature
and her living symbols. Nature is the seed of all life. When the inner powerhouse
is really operating, then you will naturally be in tune with everything else in nature.

Our ancestors recognized the advantage of working with the four elements of earth, fire, air, and water, and the planet Earth itself, for signs and signals foretelling nature's will, which directly governs man's well-being. Survival was always at the center of all life; it was the most critical and prominent focus of the day. Nature, and her omens for the future, became a powerful source of information. Nature provides a special language that can be read—when one understands the signs—from sticks and stones, flights of birds, wind directions, rain, a handful of earth, fire, or water, animal movements, or vegetation.

A simple leaf from a tree, which you hold in your hand, represents both the leaf and your being in the here and now—synchronizing with the moment of just naturally being. To our ancestors the leaf was a record, a storehouse of information that held within it the blueprint of all the years of the tree's life and the Earth before it—all of the cycles and circles of nature, bringing the tree, the Earth, and the person together in that moment.

Nature is the record of all life that has ever been, and within this record our own lives are set, and our fates and fortunes resonate.

Pyromancy
Divination by the flame

Fire is a dynamic symbol of life. It occupies a dual role, as it can be both the enemy or friend of mankind. Fire can be a blazing forest, the volcano belching its sulfurous destruction, or the searing heat of the desert. In wartime it is a crimson terror, engulfing lands and nations, but in peacetime fire is the glowing, friendly hearth, becoming a symbol of domesticity and contentment.

Fire to the ancients represented the seed of life to which all life must return. Fire symbolized the golden ray of light that materially produced heat and dryness. It was regarded as an agent of great purification and therefore of sacrifice and renewal.

From the gods
A consistent theme of mythology has been the belief that fire was stolen either from the gods or the sun and handed to man.

Sacrifices were made to the gods, placed upon the open fire. If the flame burned bright and clear, it was considered a good omen. If the flame appeared dull or noisy, spluttering as it burned, the gods were displeased and bad luck would befall the offerers. Fire remains an elementary force that can be imprisoned within a man-made cage, rigidly guarded. But it is ready, at the least relaxation of vigilance, to escape and reduce everything it encounters to ashes.

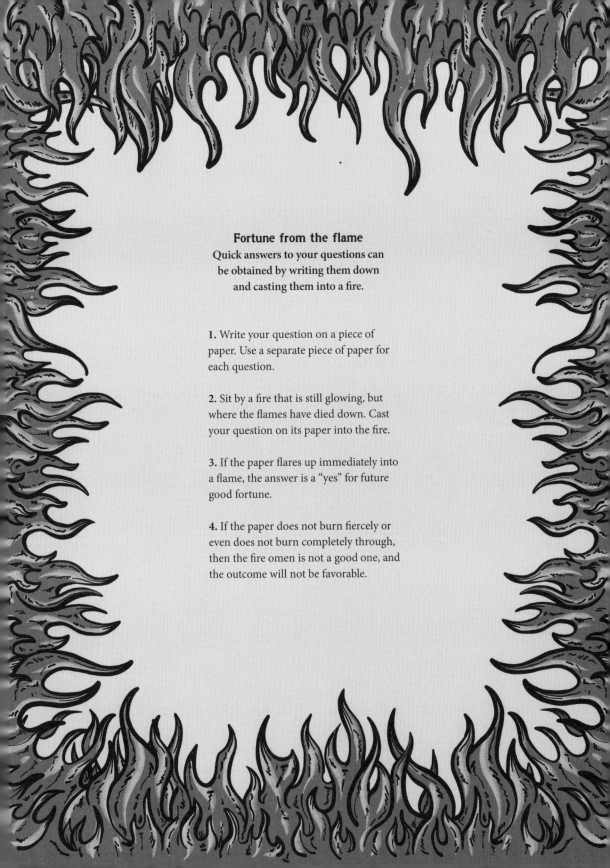

Fortune from the flame

Quick answers to your questions can
be obtained by writing them down
and casting them into a fire.

1. Write your question on a piece of
paper. Use a separate piece of paper for
each question.

2. Sit by a fire that is still glowing, but
where the flames have died down. Cast
your question on its paper into the fire.

3. If the paper flares up immediately into
a flame, the answer is a "yes" for future
good fortune.

4. If the paper does not burn fiercely or
even does not burn completely through,
then the fire omen is not a good one, and
the outcome will not be favorable.

Capnomancy

The smoke oracle

Smoke is a combination of fire and air and has always been considered a very enlightened tool to use for divination. Smoke spiraling from an opening in a roof, temple, or tepee was known as an "axis mundi," indicating a path of escape of the essences from time and space into eternal freedom.

Legend paints the picture of a human soul conceived in the flickering flame, being transformed into a spiral of smoke while moving upward to the gods. Smoke is also a reminder of the fleetingness of life.

Culture and custom

In many cultures it was customary to place incense on a fire to entice the spirits to make clear their intentions. From the appearance and behavior of the smoke that ensued, good or ill omens could be forecast.

Also used by Native Americans, smoke acted as a smudging tool to purify. A bundle of herbs was tied together and set smoldering, so that the smoke could be passed over a person or through a space, carrying away all contamination.

Smudging stick
The sweet, purifying aroma of a bunch of herbs tied together and set alight carries away unwanted energies.

Smoke prediction: will-o'-the-wisp
Divination through smoke is easily practiced in your own yard or garden. Although the description here is for an outdoor divination, it can easily be carried out indoors with the smoke from sandalwood incense.

1. In the garden, light a small fire made from wood that is slightly damp, to produce plenty of smoke.

2. Sit on the ground in front of the fire and close your eyes for a few minutes, concentrating on the question to which you would like an answer.

3. Take a deep breath in, and blow out your breath directly into the center of the smoke.

4. If the smoke moves to the right of the fire, the omen is favorable for good luck.

5. Smoke moving mainly to the left indicates a "no" to the question that has been asked—and no good fortune.

6. When the smoke shoots upward, it shows the question will not be answered by the cosmos at this particular time.

Tephramancy
Divination through ashes

Ashes have always been used for divination, especially where sacrifices were offered as a means of summoning the gods for guidance. The ashes would be carefully gathered afterward and gently scattered on the ground to see if a picture or shape appeared that could be used as a clue for fortune-telling.

The ancients saw fire in three stages. First, there was fire itself, regarded as the seed of all existing things. Next came smoke, which in folklore was used to flush any harmful nature spirits out of the forest. Finally, sacred ash remained. This was respected as the nutritious blanket of fertility on the ground, a continuous reminder of the earth's promised replenishment.

Bringer of strength
Some primitive tribes believed ashes to be the seeds of fire, falling as they do in the way that seeds of plants fall. Ashes were considered to contain great strength by the Nuba people of Southern Sudan, whose wrestlers covered themselves with ashes for extra vigor.

The year ahead
Fires for ash divination were lit on days important to the culture. The ashes were leveled when the fire was spent, and the next morning examined to see if there was anything resembling a footprint. If so, any member of the family whose foot fitted the shape would have bad luck for the next 12 months. If there was no print, or a family member's foot didn't fit, then it was a reassurance that nothing bad would affect the house or its members for the next year.

Signs in the ashes

Here's a way to use ash for your own divination technique.

1. Gather any ash that you can find and scatter it on the ground, making sure it is at least a ¼ inch (5mm) thick.

2. Close your eyes and throw onto the ash a handful of grain such as dried wheat, corn, or barley kernels.

3. Count how many grains have remained on top of the ashes. If the number is even, it's a good-luck sign; if an odd number, then your luck is "out of sight" at the moment, and it's best not to take risks for a while.

Lychnomancy and Lampadomancy

Divination by candles and the flame of a lamp

A candle flame represents light in the darkness and as such can be used to give us insight into important "yes" and "no" answers. Being easily extinguished, like life itself, it harnesses the energy force needed for prediction. Gazing at the flame of a lamp is also used as a means of divination.

Blowing out candles on a cake is an ancient ritual that we all at some time have engaged in. A child is urged to blow out all the candles in one go to assure good luck for the year ahead. Both candles and lamps can be used to divine what the future holds for us.

How to know that your partner is true

A walnut shell represents hidden wisdom, longevity, fertility, and strength in adversity.

1. You will need two halves of a walnut shell, two small candles similar to birthday candles, a bowl of water, and a match. Stand a candle upright in each half of the walnut shell by melting a little wax from another candle.

2. Set the walnut shell boats in the middle of the bowl of water, naming one candle for yourself and the other for your lover. It enhances the procedure if white candles are used to represent males and red candles for females.

3. Light the candles and repeat out loud the name of the candle for yourself, focusing on that candle and the name of your lover, while watching the other candle. If the two boats float side by side with the candles burning evenly, you will be true to each other. If the shells drift apart or fall over, or one of the flames goes out, the relationship is doomed. Whichever candle burns the longer shows that the person loves their partner more than they are loved.

Candle luck for the next year

Jack be nimble, Jack be quick, Jack jump over the candlestick! Divination rituals involving jumping over candle flames can help you to plan and be prepared for the year ahead

The candle wheel

This is best done in a garden or on a flameproof floor, and never near furnishings.

1. Place 12 white candles in a large circle. As you place each candle on the floor, light it and name it after a month of the year, beginning with January.

2. Starting with the January candle, jump over each one until you complete the circle. If any candle goes out or is knocked over, it predicts bad luck or unfortunate circumstances for that particular month. Be forewarned and take care at those times by being alert and not foolish. By the same token, all the candles that remain burning indicate good fortune for their respective months.

Pinpointing monthly adversity

When one or more of your "monthly" candles has gone out, there is a further process to pinpoint the specific area in your life that could be inharmonious in that month.

1. You will need three more candles for this: a red one, which represents your love life; a green one for money issues; and a yellow one for your career. Light all three and keep jumping over those until only one remains lit. This will be the key area to look at.

2. Repeat this for each month whose candle went out during the Candle Wheel process. Having pinpointed the specific area of your life for each month, take special precautions in that part of your life for that month.

Lampadomancy: lamp-flame gazing

Before electric light was invented, oil lamps were generally used. The flame from this became an important means of fortune-telling. The flickering light of its burning gave off many hints of good or bad omens. There are modern oil lamps available today that you can use to gain divinatory prowess.

It is important to allow the lamp to burn for at least 30 minutes before reading, so that the flame has a chance to settle. Sit down before the burning lamp, and ask your question of it. Watch carefully to see which way the flame burns.

A single straight flame points to good luck; a flame split in two foretells bad luck. If the flame bends to the right side, it shows that ill physical health could be approaching, and, if it bends to the left side, you may be in for a period of mental stress.

A flame that unusually divides into three tendrils is an exceptionally good omen, signifying extreme good fortune.

Right
A flame leaning to the right gives warning of approaching poor health.

Upright
The glow from an upright single flame points to good luck.

Split in three
A burning flame divided into three is the rarest and most fortunate omen. Good luck follows.

Left
When the flame leans to the left, extra care must be taken to avoid stress.

Split in two
When the flame is split into two, a spell of bad luck is forecast.

Your Fortune From Food

The proof of the pudding

The practice of fortune-telling from food dates back to pagan times, when, on feast days and holidays, the community would come together to plan for the future and ask what it held in store. Such traditions were absorbed into the Christian year, and, even today, the conspicuous consumption of food and drink on feast days is considered to bring good fortune.

Sweet dreams

Not surprisingly, many of the traditions and superstitions evolved around the subject of love and future lovers. On the occasion of a wedding, such thoughts were all that preoccupied the young unmarried girls present at the celebration.

One favorite method of discovering whether you will marry the man you love requires you to borrow the bride's ring and to save a small piece of the wedding cake. Pass the cake through the ring three times, each time saying his name out loud.

Write the name of your lover on a piece of turquoise-colored paper, and put it and the cake under your pillow. If the image of your heart's desire appears to you during the night, wedded bliss is assured.

Christmas cheer

Traditional Christmas cake always had a silver coin stirred into the mixture before it was cooked. A coin in your slice of cake guaranteed you good luck and fortune for the rest of the year. As solid-silver coins are hard to find today, use pure-silver jewelry charms, each of which has a slightly different meaning: a horseshoe for good fortune, a fish for fertility, a ring for a wedding, a cat for desire and good luck, and a bird for spiritual strength.

The apple of your eye

You might be familiar with the practice of reading the initials of a lover in the carefully peeled skin of an apple. You can also use an apple among a group of friends to determine who will be the first to marry. Cut one into quarters, bore a hole through each piece, and thread a line of twine through each hole,

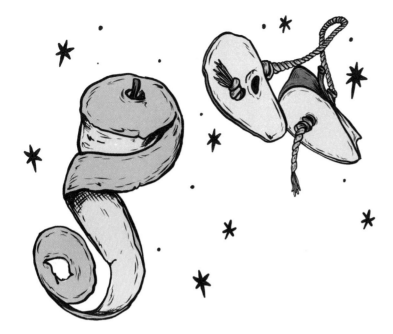

knotting it to make it secure. Each person then twirls the apple on the twine around their head and the first whose apple breaks loose and falls will be the first to wed.

Breaking eggs

On Easter Day it was customary to roll an uncooked goose or duck egg down a hill. If the egg reached the bottom without breaking, the next year promised great fortune. If you try this today in a group, paint your egg to help it stand out. You can either color your egg in a decorative fashion or color it to specify an area of life you would like the fortune to apply to: a red egg for your relationship, green for your finances, and yellow for your career.

The divining onion

Chromniomancy is the attribution of divinatory powers to onions. To find the answer to a pressing question with several possible outcomes (such as a choice of suitors) simply write each option on a piece of paper, and attach each one to a different onion. The first onion to sprout gives your answer. The most propitious place for the onions to be left to sprout used to be on a church altar, since it was believed that the spirits were more obliging in a sacred place.

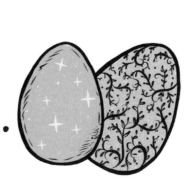

Astrology

Sent from Heaven

Astrology in its various forms is possibly the oldest form of divination. From the very earliest times, men have looked into the sky and wondered at the portents of its movements. Astrological texts over 5,000 years old have been discovered in the ruins of ancient cities such as Ur and Babylon.

Astrology does not entail any elements of the psychic—except for the intuitiveness of a good astrologer—nor of the occult or any other related phenomena. It is purely the processing and interpretation of mathematical data.

The principles

Astrology is a vast and highly complex discipline; however, the principles can be explained in enough depth so that anyone who is interested in the subject can understand how a reading is derived.

Astrology deals with the movement of the planets against their starry background. That background is divided into 12 patterns of stars, which form the signs of the zodiac. The angular relationships that the planets form, both with the signs of the zodiac and with each other, are the basis for astrological computation and interpretation.

Horoscopes to determine personality

How these computations are applied depends on how they are to be used. The most common use is in the computation—called the casting—of a natal horoscope. Although not commonly thought of as divination, the natal horoscope predicts how the person will function in various environments and the built-in strengths and weaknesses they will face life with. So, while not predicting actual events, it is certainly divination in the highest sense.

The natal horoscope records the position of the sun, moon, and planets at the moment of the person's birth within the 12 zodiac signs. Depending on the time and place of the person's birth, one of the 12 zodiac signs will be rising on the horizon—called the rising sign, or ascendant. This sign is very important since it sets the position of the houses. The houses are 12 segments of the person's life—relationships, career, health and stamina, and so on—that can be analyzed through the horoscope.

Because the Earth is constantly rotating, the position of the ascendant changes quite literally from second to second, as do the positions of the houses relative to the zodiac. It also changes by the location of the birthplace north or south of the Equator. This may sound confusing, but it can be easily visualized: the zodiac is a fixed circle of stars against which the Earth rotates. Rotating with and "attached" to the Earth are the houses.

The simplest of natal horoscopes is really not a horoscope at all, because it takes into account the position of the sun at the time of birth only. This is called your sun sign. The sun sign is important because it helps establish many significant personality factors. However, these only become fully defined when the sun sign is evaluated in combination with the large number of other planetary positions and relationships, and the position of the planets within the houses.

Life source
The sun is the center and source of all life in the solar system, and it is also at the very heart of astrology.

The signs of the zodiac and their characteristics

Aries

21 Mar–19 April

Courage; energy;
impetuosity.

Taurus

20 April–20 May

Patience; persistence;
obstinacy.

Gemini

21 May–20 June

Progressiveness;
cleverness; instability.

Cancer

21 June–22 July

Inspiration; sensitivity;
evasiveness.

Leo

23 July–22 Aug

Dignity; broad-
mindedness; power;
pretentiousness.

Virgo

23 Aug–22 Sept

Reason; logic;
exactitude; pedantry.

Libra

23 Sept–22 Oct

Harmony; evaluation;
trivialities.

Scorpio

23 Oct–21 Nov

Profundity; insistence;
roughness.

Sagittarius

22 Nov–21 Dec

Justice; propriety;
sophistry.

Capricorn

22 De–19 Jan

Independence;
abstraction;
stubbornness.

Aquarius

20 Jan–18 Feb

Spirituality; conviction;
illusion.

Pisces

19 Feb–21 Mar

Compassion; tolerance;
indolence.

Horoscopes as purely divination

The simplest use of horoscopes for divination is based purely on sun signs, which is the basis for newspaper "horoscopes." Reputable newspaper astrologers use planetary information and computations when casting sun sign horoscopes, but at best they are just shadows of full horoscopes.

A complete horoscope for divination uses the same computations as the natal horoscope, but it is computed for each individual rather than grouping the whole of humanity into just 12 groups—an obvious absurdity. It uses the positions of the planets either now or at some time in the future as a basis for forecasting future influences. "Influences" is the important word: horoscopes do not forecast events themselves but, rather, the influences on

events exerted by the positions of the planets at a particular time. Whether or not those influences are turned into actions is still entirely up to the will of the individual.

Casting a horoscope

When casting a horoscope the astrologer begins with the person's date, time, and place of birth. Using these three pieces of information, through a series of calculations the positions of the sun, moon, and planets at the moment of birth can be determined. This is done by looking up that date in an ephemeris, a book with tables of positions for the sun, moon, and planets each day. Corrections are then made for birth time to determine the ascendant.

Once the ascendant has been discovered, the positions of the 12 houses are determined and the locations of the planets in the houses can be plotted. When all the calculations have been completed and the positions of the planets established, the astrologer can begin to analyze the information that has been revealed. First, each planet is deemed to have its own characteristics that it imparts to whatever house it falls within. Next, the positions of the planets are analyzed with respect to each other to determine their aspects—the angle one planet's position makes with the position of another planet. There are five powerful aspects. The first three are considered positive aspects. They are the conjunction, where the planets involved are 0° apart—side by side; the sextile, where the planets are 60° apart; and the trine, where the planets are 120° apart. The other two aspects, the square, where the planets are 90° apart, and the opposition, where the planets are 180° apart, are considered difficult. There are a number of other aspects, but all are considered to be weaker.

With all of this information before them, the astrologer then makes a synthesis of it.

The ascendant
The casting of a full horoscope involves the computation and location of the houses relative to the position of the ascendant.

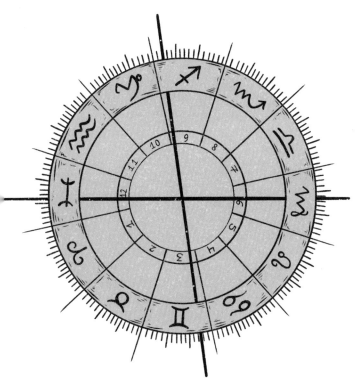

The planets and their meanings

Sun

The living being; the physical body; psychic energy; the male principle.

Moon

The soul and psyche; feeling; change and fluctuation; the feminine principle.

Mercury

Intelligence, movement; reason; communication.

Venus

Love; sex; art; physical attraction; sentimentality.

Mars

Libido; action; energy; aggression.

Jupiter

Expansion; richness; health; development.

Saturn

Contraction; limitation; inhibition; loss; parting; restriction.

Uranus

Suddenness; revolution; violence; magic, alchemy, and the occult; creativity.

Neptune

Susceptibility; fantasy; mysticism; deception; psychic abilities.

Pluto

Power; dictatorship; demagoguery.

Just as there is in life, within any horoscope there will be contradictory information, and the experience of the astrologer will come into play in determining which of the influences are active in the person's life—or, indeed, whether a combination of them is active.

For example, Mars falling in the tenth house shows a person whose pursuit of career will be energetic and powerful, possibly at the expense of other areas of his or her life. Exactly how this develops may be clarified by the influences exerted by the aspects of the planets. Should Mars in the tenth house be squared by Saturn, then the person's work life is not favorably aspected and, although that person may exert maximum effort, he or she will meet with obstacles and frustration. But, should Mars be squared by Saturn and then also be trined by Jupiter, many of Saturn's malefic influences will be rectified.

Just from this brief example of a small fragment of a horoscope, it will be seen that its interpretation is a highly complex operation. The genuine seeker should find the most skilled astrologer possible. Astrological associations exist in many countries, and their astrologers have to meet exacting standards. Most astrology publications will have resource lists for local areas.

The houses and the areas of life they represent

First
Development of personality; environment; childhood; physical body.

Second
Material possessions and money.

Third
Family relationships; communication.

Fourth
Parental home; hereditary characteristics.

Fifth
Procreation; sexuality; pleasure; risks; speculation.

Sixth
Health.

Seventh
Partnership and marriage; the community; enemies.

Eighth
Accidents; death; inheritance; marriage partner's money.

Ninth
Spiritual life; philosophy; religion; travel.

Tenth
Vocation; career; public life.

Eleventh
Hopes; wishes; friendships.

Twelfth
The unseen; secret enemies; hidden difficulties; seclusion.

Oriental Astrology

The Buddha's 12 animals

According to Chinese tradition, as the Buddha lay dying, he asked all the animals to visit him to bid him farewell. Only 12 animals appeared, and, to thank and to immortalize them, he gave each its own year. The order in which each animal appears in the Chinese zodiac is the order in which it arrived.

Oriental astrology is based on the lunar calendar, more common than solar calendars in ancient times. Each sign, signified by one of the Buddha's 12 animals, lasts for about a year. The Chinese New Year begins with the first New Moon in Aquarius, and thus can fall anywhere between early January and late February.

The signs and the animals

Because the Chinese New Year falls on a different date most years, so too do the dates of the 12 signs. Thus a person who is born in early February one year may be an Ox, but someone who is born on exactly the same date a year later would fall under the sign of the Tiger.

Each sign exerts its influence for a lunar year, until the next Full Moon in Aquarius. The 12 signs (see pages 58–61) have definite characteristics that they bestow on the personality, and each sign fares better in some years than in others.

The Rat

There is no disgrace in being a Rat in the East. It was, after all, the very first animal to answer the Buddha's call. Rats are friendly and outgoing, and always surrounded by a crowd of people. Rats have excellent instincts, and their sense of humor helps them out of scrapes when they tend to push a bit too hard. The Rat has an "easy-come, easy-go" attitude to money—until it decides it has had enough.

Favorable years Rat, Dragon, and Monkey.

Unfavorable years Rabbit, Horse, and Rooster.

Most compatible other Rats, Oxen, Dragons, Dogs, Pigs, and Monkeys.

Least compatible The rest.

The Ox

Like the animal itself, Oxen are dependable and reliable, but they can get stuck in a rut and miss out on a lot of life's pleasures. Conventional and self-sacrificing to a fault, they are not the best in family life and are not the most romantic partners. However, they are loyal and good providers, to a large degree making up for their lack of passion.

Favorable years Ox, Snake, and Rooster.

Unfavorable years Goat, Dragon, and Dog.

Most compatible Rats, other Oxen, Roosters, and Dogs.

Least compatible Tigers, Dragons, Horses, Pigs, and Monkeys

The Tiger

Tigers are one of the luckiest signs in the zodiac, and, given their tendency to take chances, it's probably just as well! They are restless, get bored easily, and are not ones for following rules. And keep them away from mirrors if you want them to get anything done!

Favorable years Tiger, Horse, and Dog.

Unfavorable years Monkey, Pig, and Snake.

Most compatible Dragons, Horses, Monkeys, and Pigs.

Least compatible Oxen, Snakes, Roosters, and Pigs.

Years of the Rat

January 24, 1936–February 10, 1937
February 10, 1948–January 28, 1949
January 28, 1960–February 14, 1961
February 15, 1972–February 2, 1973
February 2, 1984–February 19, 1985
February 19, 1996–February 6, 1997
February 7, 2008–January 25, 2009
January 25, 2020–February 11, 2021

Years of the Ox

February 11, 1937–January 30, 1938
January 29, 1949–February 16, 1950
February 15, 1961–February 4, 1962
February 3, 1973–January 22, 1974
February 20, 1985–February 8, 1986
February 7, 1997–January 27, 1998
January 26, 2009–February 13, 2010
February 12, 2021–January 31, 2022

Years of the Tiger

January 31, 1938–February 18, 1939
February 17, 1950–February 5, 1951
February 5, 1962–January 24, 1963
January 23, 1974–February 10, 1975
February 9, 1986–January 28, 1987
January 28, 1998–February 15, 1999
February 14, 2010–February 2, 2011
February 1, 2022–January 21, 2023

The Rabbit

Beauty is important to Rabbits, and they can endure extreme hardships if their surroundings are harmonious and comfortable. They will have the best of everything—whether they can afford it or not! But they are far from stuck up and distant. There is no better shoulder to cry on.

Favorable years Rabbit, Goat, and Pig.

Unfavorable years Rooster, Horse, and Rat.

Most compatible other Rabbits, Dogs, Goats, and Pigs.

Least compatible Rats, Tigers, and Horses.

The Dragon

Dragons fully live up to their name—and then wonder why people steer clear of them. You definitely don't want to upset them, unless you want singed eyebrows. Yet their strength is a wonder to behold, and they can and will carry others along when the going gets tough. Under the scaly exterior they are sentimental, loving, and affectionate, and treating them with affection turns off the flames.

Favorable years Dragon, Monkey, and Rat.

Unfavorable years Dog, Goat, and Ox.

Most compatible Rats, Dragons, Horses, and Monkeys.

Least compatible Dogs and Oxen.

The Snake

Snakes, like their namesakes, shed their skins. Often. And expensively. Their closets are full of elegant clothes, which complement their own natural attractiveness. They are surrounded by admirers—especially those who are willing to support their high-maintenance lifestyle. Noted for their indolence and double standards, nonetheless they are equally noted for their wisdom when advising others.

Favorable years Snake, Rooster, and Ox.

Unfavorable years Pig, Monkey, and Tiger.

Most compatible Oxen, Goats, and Dragons.

Least compatible Horses, Monkeys, and Pigs.

Years of the Rabbit

February 19, 1939–February 7, 1940

February 6, 1951–January 26, 1952

January 25, 1963–February 12, 1964

February 11, 1975–January 30, 1976

January 29, 1987–February 16, 1988

February 16, 1999–February 4, 2000

February 3, 2011–January 22, 2012

January 22, 2023–February 9, 2024

Years of the Dragon

February 8, 1940–January 26, 1941

January 27, 1952–February 13, 1953

February 13, 1964–February 1, 1965

January 31, 1976–February 17, 1977

February 17, 1988–February 5, 1989

February 5, 2000–January 23, 2001

January 23, 2012–February 9, 2013

February 10, 2024–January 28, 2025

Years of the Snake

January 27, 1941–February 14, 1942

February 14, 1953–February 2, 1954

February 2, 1965–January 20, 1966

February 18, 1977–February 6, 1978

February 6, 1989–January 26, 1990

January 24, 2001–February 11, 2002

February 10, 2013–January 29, 2014

January 29, 2025–February 16, 2026

The Horse

"Don't fence me in" is the horse's theme tune. They not only need to run free, but travel is at the very heart of their nature. They are great conversationalists, and are industrious and practical. Everyday tasks leave them cold, but they are the first to throw a party. They have lots of friends—on their own terms.

Favorable years Horse, Tiger, and Dog.

Unfavorable years Rat, Rabbit, and Rooster.

Most compatible Tigers, Goats, Dogs, and Pigs.

Least compatible Snakes, Monkeys, and Rabbits.

The Goat

Goats are renowned for their unconventional and creative natures, and their good taste. They are the most sympathetic sign of the zodiac but are also the most fragile. They need a great deal of tenderness from those around them, and love is at the center of their being. But don't try to hurry or push one along, or expect them to be on time!

Favorable years Goat, Rabbit, and Pig.

Unfavorable years Ox, Dragon, and Dog.

Most compatible Rabbits, other Goats, Pigs, and Monkeys.

Least compatible Rats, Tigers, and Roosters.

The Monkey

A monkey's emotions swing from happiness to dejection. If your partner is a Monkey, don't let life become too predictable—they need ups and downs to feel alive. They are the consummate fixers: If there is a way to sort out a complex situation, a Monkey will find it. But they are not above bending the truth when they deem it necessary.

Favorable years Monkey, Rat, and Dragon.

Unfavorable years Tiger, Snake, and Pig.

Most compatible Tigers, Dragons, Roosters, and Rats.

Least compatible Oxen, Snakes, and Dogs.

Years of the Horse
February 15, 1942–February 4, 1943
February 3, 1954–January 23, 1955
January 21, 1966–February 8, 1967
February 7, 1978–January 27, 1979
January 27, 1990–February 14, 1991
February 12, 2002–January 31, 2003
January 30, 2014–February 18, 2015
February 17, 2026–February 5, 2027

Years of the Goat
February 5, 1943–January 24, 1944
January 24, 1955–February 11, 1956
February 9, 1967–January 29, 1968
February 9, 1979–February 15, 1980
February 15, 1991–February 3, 1992
February 1, 2003–January 20, 2004
February 19, 2015–February 7, 2016
February 6, 2027–January 25, 2028

Years of the Monkey
January 25, 1944–February 12, 1945
February 12, 1956–January 30, 1957
January 30, 1968–February 16, 1969
February 16, 1980–February 4, 1981
February 4, 1992–January 22, 1993
January 21, 2004–February 8, 2005
February 8, 2016–January 27, 2017
January 26, 2028–February 12, 2029

The Rooster

Roosters have had more bad press—most of it undeserved—than any other sign. There is a blunt honesty about them that ruffles others' feathers. They have a tendency to give kindly advice that is often mistaken for bossiness. Roosters are natural teachers, and they have wide interests. They experience extreme ups and downs, but they always pick themselves up and carry on.

Favorable years Rooster and Snake.

Unfavorable years Rabbit, Horse, and Ox.

Most compatible Oxen, Snakes, Monkeys, and Pigs.

Least compatible Tigers, Goats, and Dogs.

The Dog

Dogs are probably the best-named signs of the zodiac. They are faithful, loyal, and affectionate, and are natural guard dogs, the fighters of injustice. Dogs respond to their surroundings: When others are up, they are up; when others are down, so are they. They tend to fight others' battles while ignoring their own.

Favorable years Dog, Horse, and Tiger.

Unfavorable years Dragon, Ox, and Goat.

Most compatible Oxen, other Dogs, and Rats.

Least compatible Dragons, Monkeys, and Goats.

The Pig

Pigs and food are a marriage made in heaven—they might as well live in the fridge! Pigs do a lot of comfort eating; they need to. They are frequently taken advantage of. They deal with harsh reality very poorly, but, when they finally snap, jump back! Pigs have hearts of gold, and in the end that is the quality that pulls them through.

Favorable years Pig, Goat, and Rabbit.

Unfavorable years Snake, Tiger, and Monkey.

Most compatible Goats, Roosters, Rabbits, and Monkeys.

Least compatible Dragons, Snakes, and Horses.

Years of the Rooster

February 13, 1945–February 1, 1946
January 31, 1957–February 17, 1958
February 17, 1969–February 5, 1970
February 5, 1981–January 24, 1982
January 23, 1993–February 9, 1994
February 9, 2005–January 28, 2006
January 28, 2017–February 14, 2018
February 13, 2029–February 2, 2030

Years of the Dog

February 2, 1946–January 21, 1947
February 18, 1958–February 7, 1959
February 6, 1970–January 26, 1971
January 25, 1982–February 12, 1983
February 10, 1994–January 30, 1995
January 29, 2006–February 16, 2007
February 15, 2018–February 4, 2019
February 3, 2030–January 22, 2031

Years of the Pig

January 22, 1947–February 9, 1948
February 8, 1959–January 27, 1960
January 27, 1971–February 14, 1972
February 13, 1983–February 1, 1984
January 31, 1995–February 18, 1996
February 17, 2007–February 6, 2008
February 5, 2019–January 24, 2020
January 23, 2031–February 10, 2032

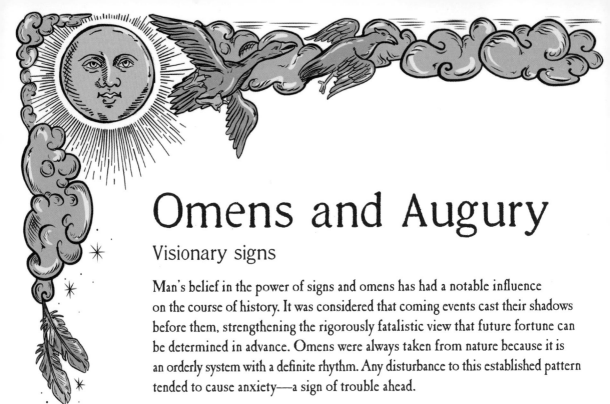

Omens and Augury

Visionary signs

Man's belief in the power of signs and omens has had a notable influence on the course of history. It was considered that coming events cast their shadows before them, strengthening the rigorously fatalistic view that future fortune can be determined in advance. Omens were always taken from nature because it is an orderly system with a definite rhythm. Any disturbance to this established pattern tended to cause anxiety—a sign of trouble ahead.

As in the past, an omen predicts a fortunate future, or gives warnings of dangers to be avoided; but omens can always be taken as signals of opportunities to be seized. All that is required is that we take notice of the elements of the natural world around us.

The augur: the omen interpreter

Throughout history an augurist was an expert trained to consult the omens to make predictions by reading the wishes of the gods, expressed through nature. They took

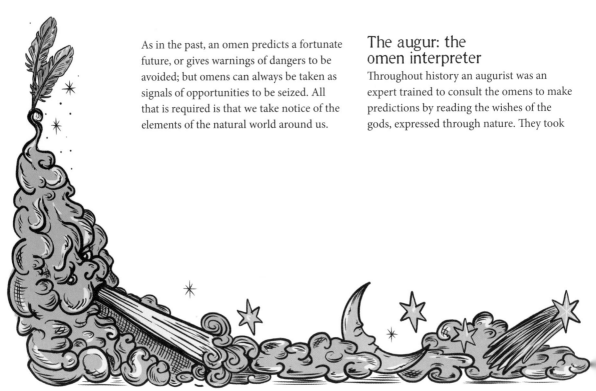

omens from any area of life, from the most mundane daily activities to the omens of shooting stars—meteormancy. Birds were often of particular interest to the augurists, who drew their omens from the shedding of feathers and the arrangement and consistency of bird droppings. The augur selected possible outcomes to natural events and then whichever outcome succeeded was interpreted as a sign from nature.

To enhance your own abilities as an augurist, you should wear ecclesiastical purple and pagan orange, and clasp in your right hand an arm's-length staff made from an unaltered tree branch.

Omens of the sky

A fruitful source of omens is the sky, with its stars, sun, wind, rain, and the direction of flights of birds. For example, a single or flock of birds flying to the right is an omen

of monetary gains, or a good harvest. Flying to the left foretells spiritual enlightenment.

Austromancy: answers from the air

Reading omens from the air is simplified by cutting two pieces of paper to the same size and weight, one red and one blue. From an open window, drop both pieces into the wind. The red piece is a "yes" answer to whatever question you have in mind, and the blue is a "no." Whichever piece reaches the ground first is your answer.

Hydromancy: omens in the deep

With a question in mind, throw a black pebble into a pond or standing water and count the ripples. An odd number means the answer is "yes"; an even number means "no."

Animal omens

Both wild and domestic animals have always made an immense contribution to omen law. Early man, and especially the Egyptians, recognized a close link between themselves and the beasts, which they feared, used, or admired. They designed magical methods to obtain the animals' powers, and elevated some animals to the realms of the gods. Many of the ancient gods were depicted as human forms with animal heads.

Throughout history various animals have had different meanings. A classic example is the cat—revered as sacred in ancient Egypt. Cat cemeteries containing thousands of felines have been found. They were so revered that to injure a cat could result in the death penalty. In medieval Europe cats were believed to be the consorts of witches and, as such, suffered the same fate—they were burned alive!

Horses

A white horse seen in dreams is the sender of ill luck—once believed to possibly even foretell a forthcoming death. But a white horse viewed by lovers is a fortunate sign for the future relationship. A black horse is a sign of good luck. A piebald horse—the two-colored animal—is an exceptionally good omen.

Cats

A cat following you is good fortune. A cat washing its face indicates rain. A black cat is considered good luck in the UK but in some parts of the USA and Europe it is considered an ill omen. A cat crossing your path brings in good luck, but only if it crosses over from your right to left.

Dogs

The appearance of a small dog spells good luck, while the appearance of three white dogs indicates extreme abundance. A stray dog following you home brings in good fortune—especially for the dog if you take it in!

Birds

The cuckoo is regarded as the bringer of spring and new life. It indicates by its call what the future holds for you. If you hear it from your right side the first time you hear it in the spring, it is a good omen; if its first call comes from your left side, there are troubles ahead.

Animal entrails and organs

Divination from the appearance of the entrails from animals was practiced by the Assyrians, Babylonians, Romans, Aztecs, and the Africans, mainly from animals sacrificed to the gods.

Liver examination

Prediction by the liver was highly regarded in ancient times, because it was considered by many to be the seat of life. All the veins, marks, and spots in the liver had specific meaning. The liver was sectioned in 55 zones, each relating to a specific god. A clay model found in Babylon dated between the nineteenth and sixteenth centuries B.C. could have been used for teaching students.

Diverse sources of omens

Omens are not only found in the natural world but also in our own self-created environments of home and garden. The body provides indications of things to come, too.

Home omens

The home generates its own particular omens. A broken mirror signals seven years of bad luck. Any changes in the rhythm of a clock in the home are ominous; in the past it was believed that this could even mean death. Scissors dropped on the floor indicate disappointment, but scissors hanging on a hook reveal good luck. Crossed knives on a table are omens of bad luck, while knives given as a gift at a wedding are good luck if accompanied by a coin.

Garden omens

Bees are traditionally bearers of good will from the very lap of the gods. If a swarm settles in your garden, prosperity is surely bound to follow.

Finding a spider on you is considered good fortune. A small red spider indicates money ahead. A spider spinning a web indicates plans being made for the future, which can be good or bad. Killing a spider turns the tide of your life to ill fortune.

Nine peas found in a pod proclaims good fortune indeed. Finding a four-leaf clover is a long-standing omen of good luck, and a worm found in an apple prophesies an intruder into your good fortune.

Body omens

Itches and tingling of the body are happy or unhappy omens, depending whether they are on the right- or left-hand side of the body: the right-hand side is fortunate; the left-hand side is a worry. Itching on the soles of the feet indicates that a trip abroad is imminent. To trip or stumble implies unfortunate prospects for projects at hand or for the future in general.

Chapter 3
Reading Objects

If your preference when divining is to work with one specific object, when your personal power is activated everything in the outer universe speaks to you. The most sacred object of all in ancient times was the chalice—known as the "cup of salvation," because it was said to give forth continual abundance.

All objects are matter, which is solidified essence. This makes them great conductors for "tuning in." Everything emits energy, be it thought, emotion, or action. The sea and air, human beings, and animals can be read and used for reference in fortune-telling. But even so-called inanimate objects exude information when you become sensitive enough to pick up the messages from their signals. Everything on Earth has its own special vibration, and as such can be sensed by the reader to gain access to the divine.

The article used in the reading process is called an inductor. Through it you have a way of receiving extrasensory indications—known as object reading. The specific name given to the gifted person's ability to read objects is paragnosis. Amazing detail can be picked up by a clairvoyant from merely touching a cup or a scarf belonging to the client, which has, in some way, recorded the circumstances that were experienced by the object.

The strength of the messages that manifest themselves through objects is illustrated by the fact that objects sometimes disappear and reappear, removing themselves to unlikely places only to be found again later, back in the same position.

Scrying

Divining with a crystal ball

To scry is "to see into the future" by peering into any reflective surface—whether water, a mirror, or a crystal—for a vision of things yet to be. Scrying has been practiced for centuries all over the world.

Just about every culture has, at some point, employed various forms of scrying for divination. Michel de Notredame, or Nostradamus (1503–1566), whose prophecies included the Great Fire of London in 1666, the French Revolution, and the atom bomb, is perhaps the most famous scryer of all time.

Summoning visions

Find a quiet, uncluttered room, and make sure it is spotlessly clean—dust hinders psychic phenomena. Draw the shades, and allow only the dimmest candlelight. It is best not to have more than one person for a sitting and they should sit opposite you, the scryer.

Acquiring a good-quality crystal ball is essential if you are determined to become a serious student of the "mysteries of the clouds" upon which scrying is based. To prepare the ball, cleanse it in a little white vinegar and tepid water; then polish it dry with chamois leather.

Focusing the energies

Put the ball on its stand, steady your mind, and look deeply into the glass. Indistinct images resembling swirling clouds will soon start to appear, usually through a milky-white hue. It is rare to get whole scenes or pictures straightaway—only the gifted psychic will do so—but a misty impression is often all that is needed to lead you in.

As you get more involved in your scrying, the clouds and images will begin to assume colors as well as shapes. Each color lends a different interpretation (see page 70). With practice you will start to discern well-defined images within the clouds. It is these that will give you your most accurate readings.

Cloud color
White clouds indicate peace and contentment while black warn of certain troubles ahead. Red or yellow shapes encourage action—the auspices are good. Blue or indigo are the colors of wisdom and self-development, while green indicates security in matters of both love and finance.

Cloud colors interpretations

Take into account other colors that may appear along with traditionally seen black and white clouds.

Black and white clouds

Black and white are usually the first colors to be seen: white for peace and contentment; black for possible troubles ahead. Allow the mist to transform and take shape to reveal shapes, symbols, or even pictures.

Green clouds

Money should not be a problem. Pay attention to relationships and encourage love. It is a prosperous time for the home.

Red, orange, and yellow clouds

A lot of energy will be needed if endeavors are to come to fruition. Look before you leap. Life should be on the move—not static. Health is good.

Blue, indigo, and violet clouds

These colors indicate a time to reconsider and structure your life in a positive manner. If careful planning is followed, you may acquire all that is desired; but be careful not to get stuck in a rut.

Moving clouds interpretations

As the clouds swirl and move in your crystal ball, the direction of these psychic mists will give specific answers to "yes" and "no" questions. When shown colored, these silent pictures give extra information to the fortune-teller.

Cloud direction	Black and white	Green	Red, orange, and yellow	Blue, indigo, and purple
Ascending	"Yes" to any questions.	Life is good; a period of stability.	Extreme, positive activity.	The necessary wisdom and experience are now available. Aim for self-employment.
Descending	"No" to any questions.	Money is going out faster than it is coming in.	Can show you are being careless and slapdash, leading to a nasty fall from life's position. Closure to a project is nearer than you think.	Loss of opportunities and disappointment here. May have delusions of grandeur.
Moving to the left	Positive energy about to move away.	The money is running out. Others are jealous of you.	It's too late. Opportunities have been missed. Expect cancellations.	Definitely not the time to push forward or to ask for a promotion.
Moving to the right	A good omen, support is at hand.	A comfortable time.	Results come quickly.	A good time to stand up and be recognized.

The Pendulum

Amplifying the hidden forces

The use of the pendulum is an offshoot of divining, where a dowser uses a forked twig held out in front of him by both hands. A mysterious force pulls down the third end when the stick is moved over the land, indicating water, minerals, or buried treasure in the ground below.

The practice of dowsing was transferred to indoors and became known as the "pendulum force," where a similar unseen power exerts itself and the pendulum acts as an amplifier. The dowsing rod was said to represent the witch's broomstick. The first pendulums were also made of wood because of their association with the dowsing rod.

Pendulums then and now

The first wooden pendulums were carved in a teardrop shape from the orrisroot, used because of its potent connection to the earth spirits. It was suspended from a fine chain or piece of string, allowing it to swing around at will. Hazel and ash were also regarded as magical woods.

Modern pendulums can be made of wood, crystal, silver, or gold. Any item is appropriate that will fit at the end of a 12-inch (30cm) piece of chain—or even a button on the end of a piece of cotton thread will suffice.

Pendulum colors

A colored pendulum is generally more potent than a black or white one, with certain colors relating to specific life areas. For example, if your question relates to travel, children, or your sex life, use a red pendulum. The color energy within the pendulum will direct the unseen forces.

Red
Travel; sex life; children; motherhood; growth.

Orange
Work; divorce; career opportunities; social contacts.

Yellow
The media; intellectual accomplishments; examinations.

Green
Romance; marriage; money; finance; general health.

Blue
The healer; literary opportunities; questions of discretion.

Indigo
House moves; psychic potential.

Purple
Leadership qualities; artistic possibilities; self-employment.

Pendulum technique

The pendulum is useful for foretelling future events or answering those urgent questions. Use this method to harness your extrasensory perception, which is the unconscious act of subliminal phenomenon.

1. Acquire a pendulum of your choice and make sure it is suspended by a piece of string, cotton, or chain.

2. Hold the end of the chain between the first finger and thumb of either hand.

3. Place the pendulum over the outstretched palm of the other hand, about 2 inches (5cm) above the palm.

4. When the pendulum is dead steady, in your mind, speak to the spirits by saying: "If it so pleases you to answer me . . ." Then ask your question. Be certain the question you ask can be answered with "yes" or "no." Ask only one question at a time to avoid confusion.

5. Wait and see if the pendulum swings to the right in a circle, which means "yes," or to the left, which means "no." Moving backward and forward indicates that no answer will be given—it doesn't know—or that it is not possible to offer an answer at the present time.

Give thanks

If you sincerely ask questions of the spirits through the pendulum, you will find an answer. The spirit of the universe should always be thanked for whatever it reveals —failing to give this courtesy weakens the link so that the connection the next time will be weaker.

Using a pendulum
Hold the pendulum at the end of the chain to allow a full swing to take place without hindrance.

Color Divination
Color wheel of destiny

A good way to access your intuitiveness is to use a pendulum in conjunction with the color wheel of fortune. Throughout ancient history, color was harnessed as an aid for divination. The ancients were fully aware that a person's intuitive capacity is increased by the use of color, simply through harnessing its vibrations: thinking, seeing, or visualizing it.

The rainbow's energetic force is part of our psychic makeup. Each color vibrates at its own particular rate, a vibration that can awaken your fortune-telling ability. Color will pinpoint the next step that is necessary for you to act upon; it becomes a lead-in, a guide for your endeavors.

Color wheel technique

You will need a clear crystal pendulum on a thread or chain. The brilliant, pure crystal will act as a touch of the sun's cosmic light. It contains all the spectrum colors, enabling a purity of quest as it resonates internally, laying bare all before it in the transparency of the cosmic light.

1. Place your pendulum in the center of the color wheel opposite. Consider what it is you wish to know and slowly ask your question.

2. Allow the pendulum to swing backward and forward until it moves, freely settling onto only one color segment.

3. Now bring in your fortune-telling ability to interpret your psychic color key, using the Interpretation Guide, opposite, to reveal which aspect of your life the color has shown you.

4. There are several words associated with each color. Meditate with each of the words in turn to see which one (or ones) you need to focus on. If you are working with your intuitive powers, you will get a sense with each word whether it is "yes" or "no."

5. To find more clarity in the areas shown, ask further questions, with each successive question giving a closer definition of the answer. Each additional question may draw you to yet another color, so you will need to work with the interpretations of the new color or colors.

Color wheel

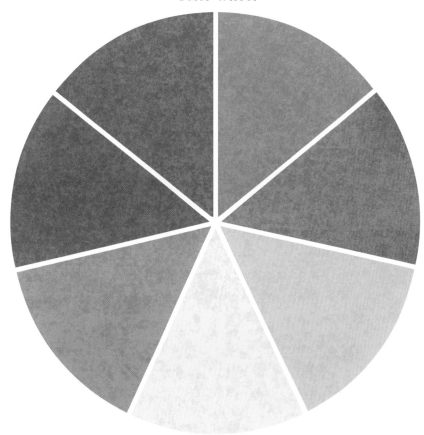

Interpretation guide

Purple
Protector; self-employed;
perception; teacher.
Physical Brain.

Indigo
Unravels the unknown;
structure; preparation.
Physical Skeleton;
the bones.

Red
Love; sex energy
levels; physical
stamina; expansion.
Physical Circulation
of the blood.

Orange
Break-ups;
changes; opportunities;
gentle stimulation.
Physical Kidneys.

Yellow
Alertness; flexibility;
career; media; eloquency.
Physical Stomach.

Green
Harmony; prosperity;
giver; dependable;
relationships.
Physical Heart.

Blue
Tranquillity; truth;
integrity; peace with
a purpose.
Physical Throat.

Psychometry

Divining through the sense of touch

Psychometry is one of the most easily acquired psychic skills used for fortune-telling. It is the instant-touch technique for reading past, present, and future events from ordinary objects such as clothing and jewelry. It takes time, patience, and sensitivity—but can be very rewarding.

Psychometry requires nothing more than an item that belongs to the person who seeks enlightenment. The item has to be something of an intimate nature that has been worn or used, so that vibrations and impressions can be picked up from it, enabling the reader to tune in to the psychic realm.

Requisites

Certain requisites need to be employed to receive information: an object, time, patience, and the capacity to tune in to your intuitive, clairvoyant ability. The psychometrist will need to meditate on the object until the past, present, or future events are revealed about the owner. To gain access to information you can simply scan an object with your fingertips to pick up its past exposure to knowledge and experience—the object becomes your lead into the unexplored and the unknown.

Practice this simple art and eventually you will not need to touch anything: the advanced psychometrist will be able to receive impressions merely at a glance, or even receive an impression from the briefest of handshakes. This method can also be employed when visiting a historical home, or even a friend's house. We all do this unconsciously, anyway: it is called the "atmosphere" of a place.

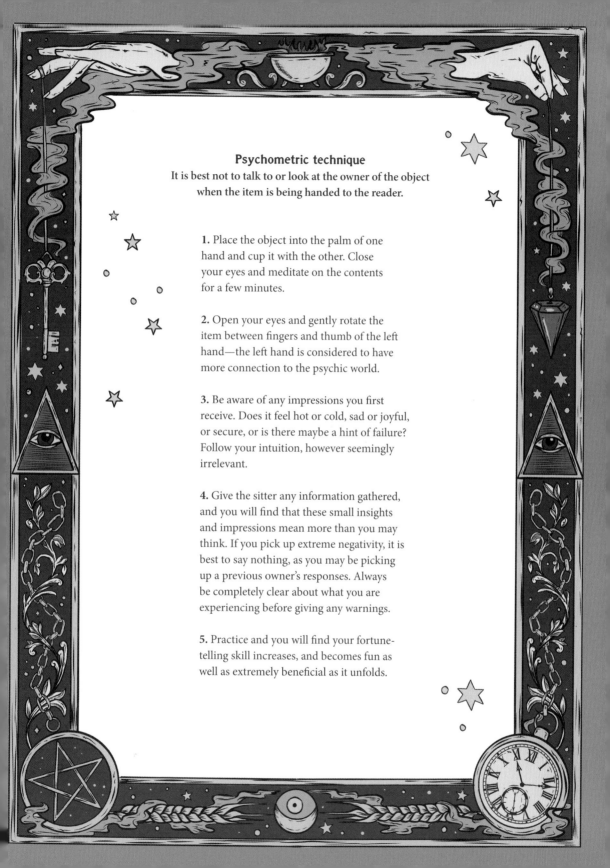

Psychometric technique

It is best not to talk to or look at the owner of the object when the item is being handed to the reader.

1. Place the object into the palm of one hand and cup it with the other. Close your eyes and meditate on the contents for a few minutes.

2. Open your eyes and gently rotate the item between fingers and thumb of the left hand—the left hand is considered to have more connection to the psychic world.

3. Be aware of any impressions you first receive. Does it feel hot or cold, sad or joyful, or secure, or is there maybe a hint of failure? Follow your intuition, however seemingly irrelevant.

4. Give the sitter any information gathered, and you will find that these small insights and impressions mean more than you may think. If you pick up extreme negativity, it is best to say nothing, as you may be picking up a previous owner's responses. Always be completely clear about what you are experiencing before giving any warnings.

5. Practice and you will find your fortune-telling skill increases, and becomes fun as well as extremely beneficial as it unfolds.

Chapter 4
Revelations of the Random

A time may come when the reader wants to widen their fortune-telling horizons, and expand into deeper levels of intuition and clairvoyance. The techniques of this section provide that opportunity. This part touches the most basic and ancient part of us, going back to the very beginnings of divination itself.

The casting of lots, earth, runes—in fact anything that leaves the hand and falls or is placed into a position to be read—has always played a significant part in predicting man's destiny. Scattering to the winds was embraced by all cultures from the earliest civilizations. Whatever was at hand was given the freedom of the wind, picking up the same divine forces that imbue the air itself.

Some of the earliest records refer to messages from the bones. Bones, being the framework of the body and the part that lasts the longest, were regarded as the root of life, and became a natural tool of divination and fortune-telling. The methods and techniques that followed, from the casting of bones to more sophisticated methods such as the *I Ching*, were all derived from "casting fate to the wind."

In Africa, bushmen and witch doctors were individuals recognized as having heightened powers of perception, putting them into the position of being the social advisers of their tribe. The practice of bula—bone throwing—was the means of consulting the spirits about important tribal matters. The patterns formed when the bones were thrown were believed to reveal the future. In a like manner, there was a belief in some cultures of "the serenity of the stones," specifically marked stones and pebbles cast for the same purposes as the bones, and all having their origins in "bone casting."

Geomancy
Significance in the soil

Divination by the soil is known as geomancy. Divinatory significance is drawn from patterns and symbols that have formed by random scattering, to connect to the spirits of earth, sand, or dust. Here we look at active and passive sand casting.

Fortune-telling by sand reading is as old as the hills. Crabs, and insects such as beetles, were allowed to roam freely over thrown sand leaving their footprints and markings to be consulted, revealing sacred messages from the gods.

There are two methods of sand reading that can be used to gain future insights.

Passive sand casting
This method is for personal messages. You will need some fine, dry sand spread out onto a smooth, even surface such as a kitchen table. Hold a twig—about the length of a pen—in your hand.

1. Close your eyes and take in a few deep breaths to help you concentrate on the open space above your head. Allow the thoughts and feelings from this space to travel through your head and down your arm into the twig.

2. Let the twig move over the sand at will.

3. When you feel the twig has stopped, open your eyes and read the signs from your sacred writing. Letters may have formed. An "N" could be interpreted as a "no," a "Y" could indicate a future "yes" for good fortune. To go beyond the individual symbols, try to see if a picture has formed, giving you a scene, a "lens-eye view" into the future.

Active color sand casting

This method is used when forecasting for another person. You will need a flat, clean surface and several small bowls of sand mixed with powder paint. If the person wants to know about relationships, mix the sand with red powder paint. Use orange sand for physical fitness, and yellow for work prospects. Green sand is used for money issues, blue will reveal the truth regarding any situation, and purple sand is used for self-employment and assessing the person's psychic abilities.

1. Use the sitting as a forecast for one year ahead. The person throwing the sand will be the reader. Throw a handful of colored sand so that it streams across the surface of the table. The vibrations from the color in the sand will answer questions regarding love aspects.

2. Look also at shapes and symbols that have formed for fortune-telling predictions.

Symbol interpretations

There are five major symbols that regularly appear. These are drawn from ancient alchemical teachings. See the interpretations below.

Square

A closed square means great protection—the positive will overcome the negative. If your square is open at one corner you are vulnerable at the moment.

Cross

A right-angle cross implies future upheavals and disruption.

Chain

Chains could indicate bad luck. Each link of the chain represents several months of struggle.

Fork

A fork shows a crossroad in one's life. If the right-hand branch is longer, it leads to extreme good fortune.

Circle

A circle is general good luck.

The Runes

Divining from "the bones"

According to Norse mythology, the great god Odin—who rode through the sky on an eight-legged horse accompanied by a wolf—hung for nine days and nights without food and water impaled on his own spear from the great world tree known as *Yggdrasil*. He endured this torture for the purpose of gaining for his people knowledge of the runes.

From the second century AD the Norse Masters of the Runes used them to predict future events or for healing, controlling the weather, and protecting. They could be engraved on swords to enhance warriors' abilities, and they were worn on amulets to draw love, prosperity, and happiness.

Using the runes

The magical associations of runes became a prominent component of German belief in the years preceding 1939, but historians and rune experts alike condemn these interpretations. Runes can either be bought in sets, or you can make your own. They can be burned into small, rectangular pieces of wood (as the Norse Rune Masters did), or painted or engraved on flat stones, pieces of metal, or even on small rectangles of cardboard. They are engraved on only one side—the other remains blank. In ancient times these were often referred to as "bones," tying them to the even more ancient practice described in the opening of this chapter.

Casting the runes

Casting the runes originally meant that they were "thrown at" the person seeking counsel through them. They were the physical part of a magic spell being worked through them, a bridge between the conscious and subconscious of the seeker.

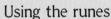

Casting method

There are various methods of casting and interpreting the runes in use today. The following method is a common one:

1. It is said that an invocation to Odin before casting the runes is beneficial in preventing the intervention of malefic spirits! For example, say "Oh great Odin, guide my hand."

2. Have a specific question in mind, and the time period during which you are asking to see the influences relating to your question. It can be a day, a month, a year, or even the next hour!

3. Scatter the runes face down in front of you. Should any fall face up, turn them over, and mix them back into the remainder with your eyes closed, so you will not recognize where they are when you open your eyes.

4. Choose 13, and arrange them in a circle in the order chosen, with the last rune placed in the center, as in the diagram below. The runes are in the upright position when their tops face the center of the circle.

5. Use the interpretations detailed on pages 84–85 to read the insights you have been given.

The runic wheel

The runic wheel spread is also known as the horoscope formation. Each position, from one to 12, represents an area of the inquirer's life (see The Houses, page 55). The thirteenth rune represents the inquirer—sometimes called the Querant. This thirteenth rune signifies the trend that will affect the Querant most during the time period for which the cast is being made.

Each rune relates to the ones on either side, showing the overlapping influences in effect during the time period for which the cast is being made. When malefic influences are shown by casting a *yfelrun*, a "bad" rune, the consequences can often be avoided by not performing the action that the rune warns against—most of these runes are a warning not to undertake a specific action.

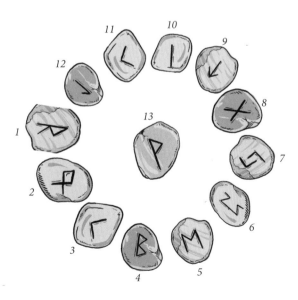

Runes and their meanings

	Feoh	Ur	Thorn	As
Upright	Wealth; love is fulfilled.	Stamina; promotion at work.	Defense; protection; caution.	Good advice from elders.
Reversed	Loss of wealth or love.	Missed opportunities.	Wrong decision; overcaution.	Be wary of poor advice.

	Nyd	Is	Ger	Eoh
Upright	Plan carefully; be patient.	An impediment; cooling off; a situation is frozen.	Ending and renewal; effort is rewarded.	Endings; emotional difficulties; growth and change.
Reversed	Avoid change; delay decisions.	No reverse.	No reverse.	No reverse.

	Eow	Man	Lagu	Ing
Upright	Journeys; a change of home or work.	Charity; altruism; humanity.	Intuition; premonition.	Good news; a stranger comes into your life; family.
Reversed	Enemies; unexpected travel.	Isolation; detachment.	Emotional turmoil; paranoia.	No reverse.

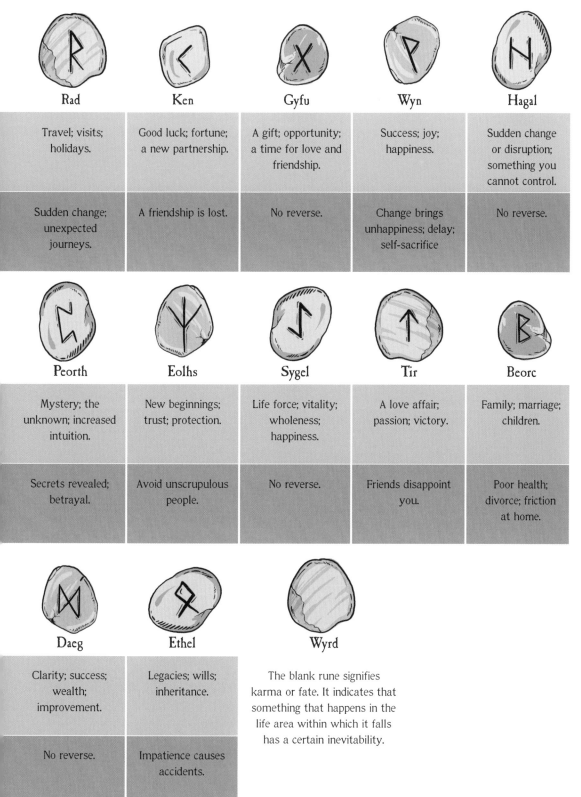

Rad	Ken	Gyfu	Wyn	Hagal
Travel; visits; holidays.	Good luck; fortune; a new partnership.	A gift; opportunity; a time for love and friendship.	Success; joy; happiness.	Sudden change or disruption; something you cannot control.
Sudden change; unexpected journeys.	A friendship is lost.	No reverse.	Change brings unhappiness; delay; self-sacrifice	No reverse.

Peorth	Eolhs	Sygel	Tir	Beorc
Mystery; the unknown; increased intuition.	New beginnings; trust; protection.	Life force; vitality; wholeness; happiness.	A love affair; passion; victory.	Family; marriage; children.
Secrets revealed; betrayal.	Avoid unscrupulous people.	No reverse.	Friends disappoint you.	Poor health; divorce; friction at home.

Daeg	Ethel	Wyrd
Clarity; success; wealth; improvement.	Legacies; wills; inheritance.	The blank rune signifies karma or fate. It indicates that something that happens in the life area within which it falls has a certain inevitability.
No reverse.	Impatience causes accidents.	

The *I Ching*
Revelations from *The Book of Changes*

The *I Ching* is one of the most ancient of oracles, dating back at least 4,000 years. It is derived from Eastern philosophy, which recognizes that all that exists in the world is composed of opposite but complementary forces—the Yin (the female principle: dark, mysterious, negative) and the Yang (the male principle: active, heavenly, positive).

The *I Ching* oracle is based on the understanding that all things are interconnected, and that, in the casting of lots with a specific question in mind, the fall of the objects will in some way reflect the forces at work in the person's life.

Interpreting *The Book of Changes*

In the *I Ching*, properly called *The Book of Changes*, the Yin principle is represented by a single, unbroken line (____), and the Yang by a broken line (__ __). Broken lines are considered to be yielding, while unbroken lines are firm. Yin and Yang lines and their principles are arranged into groups of three, called trigrams. There are eight basic combinations of Yin and Yang trigrams, which represent all that happens in Heaven and Earth. The most common meanings for each are shown opposite.

Casting the *I Ching*

To begin, have the question in mind for which you are seeking the answer. The more specific the question, the clearer the answer. To divine through the *I Ching*, two groups of trigrams are cast, using either yarrow sticks or coins. The coin method is given here, because it can be done with ordinary coins.

1. First, decide whether "heads" or "tails" is Yin; the opposite side is Yang. Throw a coin in the air three times. If Yang comes up twice the line is Yang; if Yin comes up twice the line is Yin. You now have the first line of the first trigram. Write them down as you throw them.

2. Repeat Step 1 twice more to complete the first trigram—the Upper Trigram.

3. Repeats Steps 1–2 to complete the second trigram—the Lower Trigram.

4. Two trigrams together combine to make 64 different hexagrams. Use the table on page 92 to find the number of your hexagram and find its interpretation on pages 93–99.

5. If three Yin or Yang coins come up, the line is a "moving" line, indicating a state of fluctuation: the Yin line will become a Yang, and vice versa. If you get a moving line, read the interpretation for the hexagram with its original Yin or Yang meaning first, then read the interpretation for what it will become when the Yins become Yangs, or vice versa. This indicates what changes are going to occur, if any.

Throws for the Upper Trigram

A throwing example
In this case "heads" was Yin. The Upper Trigram is Ch'ien and the Lower Trigram is K'an. The number of the hexagram is 6.

Throws for the Lower Trigram

The eight trigrams

As well as working in combination to make the hexagrams, each trigram also has its own associations.

Ch'ien
Heaven; father; sky; creative; strong; active; firm; light; cold.

Tui
Lake; marsh; rain; fall; youngest daughter; joyful; pleasure

Li
Fire; lightning; sun; summer; middle daughter; beautiful; clinging.

Chen
Thunder; spring; eldest son; activity; movement; arousing.

Sun
Wind; wood; eldest daughter; gentle; penetrating.

K'an
Water; cloud; a pit; moon; winter; middle son; dangerous; enveloping.

Ken
Mountain; thunder; youngest son; stubborn; perverse; immovable.

K'un
Earth; heat; mother; receptive; responsible; passive; yielding; weak; dark.

Hexagram numbers

Upper Trigram →	CH'IEN	CHEN	K'AN	KEN	K'UN	SUN	LI	TUI
Lower Trigram ↓								
CH'IEN	1	34	5	26	11	9	14	43
CHEN	25	51	3	27	24	42	21	17
K'AN	6	40	29	4	7	59	64	47
KEN	33	62	39	52	15	53	56	31
K'UN	12	16	8	23	2	20	35	45
SUN	44	32	48	18	46	57	50	28
LI	13	55	63	22	36	37	30	49
TUI	10	54	60	41	19	61	38	58

Hexagram interpretations

Find your hexagram number using the table left, and discover the interpretation over the next few pages. If a month is mentioned in the interpretation it indicates when an event may take place.

1. Ch'ien: creativity
Success through creativity; danger easily overcome; May.

2. K'un: passivity
Success after difficulty; determination is needed; November.

3. Chun: difficult beginnings
Difficulty followed by success; not the time to start something new; December.

4. Meng: immaturity
Good luck! Have patience; give advice only when asked; January.

5. Hsu: waiting
Sit back and let the future take its natural course; February.

6. Sung: conflict
Situation cannot be successfully resolved—give up; do not travel; March.

7. Shih: the army
Life's battle—progress with a difficult or dangerous task wins you respect; April.

8. Pi: unity
Cooperation brings progress; consult the oracle further; April.

9. Hsiao ch'u: the lesser nourisher
Things run smoothly but not yet time to take further action; April.

10. Lu: treading
Dangerous present situation, so be cautious; you are likely to succeed; June.

11. T'ai: peace
Present difficulties can be overcome; draw on inner strength; February.

12. P'i: stagnation
Obstruction; disharmony and weakness; August.

13. T'ung jen: universal brotherhood
Lovers; friends; accept the situation for what it is; not the time to complain; July.

14. Tayu: great possessions
Cultural achievement; fantastic success; good triumphs over evil; May.

15. Ch'ien: modesty
Only things that add to the general good are successful; December.

16. Yu: enthusiasm
Proceed if you are certain that the present action is the right one; March.

17. Sui: following
Accept only what you know to be right; beware of ulterior motives.

18. Ku: decay
Ruined work; the end is only a new beginning; March.

19. Lin: approach
Great success will follow if things are put right; January.

20. Kuan: contemplation
Decide whether you are following the right path; take a hard look at your life; September.

21. Shih ho: gnawing
Success in legal proceedings; you are not to blame; October.

22. Bi: elegance

Chance; good luck; a time for watching and learning; August.

23. Po: Separating

Get rid of hindrances; no goal can be pursued successfully now; October.

24. Fu: Return

Self-discipline and kindness to others are necessary; friends arriving; December.

25. Wu Wang: The Unexpected

Only those who do what is right can expect to succeed; September.

26. Ta ch'u: the great nourisher

Good for travel; success only if you persevere with what is right; August.

27. I: nourishment

Consistent effort brings good success; November.

28. Ta kuo: excess

Have a firm goal in mind to supplement any weakness in plans; October.

29. K'an: the abyss

Great danger. Keep a tight rein on the mind to prevent illusion and fear; period from November to January.

30. Li: fire

Good fortune can be gained by looking after those who need help. Clear the mind; period from May to July.

31. Hsien: influence

Good fortune will result from taking a partner; persistence brings rewards; May.

32. Heng: duration

The long enduring; success through perseverance and freedom from error; July.

33. Tun: retreat

No great achievement now; persist only in small things; pay attention to detail; July.

34. Ta chuang: the power of the great

Only the strong and persistent wield power; get out of comfortable rut; March.

35. Chin: progress

Merit is rewarded; do not push on blindly; be generous.

36. Ming i: darkening of the light

Steadfastness in the face of difficulty; hide your light under a bushel for the moment; September.

37. Chia jen : the family

Put family happiness above personal happiness.

38. K'uei: opposition

Do not be encouraged to do too much; take pleasure in the small things; December.

39. Chien: trouble

Difficulties lie ahead, but do not take the easy and dishonest way out; November.

40. Hsieh: release

Those with nothing to gain from present plans should give them up; those with much to gain should speed things up.

41. Sun: reduction

Loss at first, but success is ahead; not a good time for marriage or business; July.

42. I: gain

Good fortune; past actions are now bringing benefits; January.

43. Kuai: breakthrough

Do not take on difficult tasks through vanity; trust only those you are sure of; April.

44. Kou: contact
All types of business and social contact, meetings, and so on; present difficulty can be overcome by persistence and caution; June.

45. Ts'ui: gathering
Get together to sort things out; make some sort of sacrifice; March.

46. Sheng: promotion
Timing is important now; take things slowly and unexpected good luck will help you; December.

47. K'un: exhaustion
Not a good omen as any trouble is mostly self-made; September.

48. Ching: a well
Do only that which is practical; May.

49. Ko: revolution
Before there is any progress radical changes must be made.

50. Ting: sacrificial urn
Obligations and duties should be fulfilled as gracefully as possible; a missed opportunity could cause trouble; June.

51. Chen: thunder
Powerful beneficial forces are in action now; October.

52. Ken: keeping still
Time for action and a time for rest, to be sure you are doing the right thing; period from February to April.

53. Chien: gradual progress
Constant but gradual movement is the best; fulfillment of desires; January.

54. Kuei mei: the marrying maiden
Usually an unfortunate omen; advancement now would be disastrous; September.

55. Feng: abundance
May indicate too much of a good thing; the tide of fortune or misfortune can quickly change; June.

56. Lu: the traveler
No loss in traveling; small matters will be successful; April.

57. Sun: willing submission
Success to those who adapt; visit a great or wise man; August.

58. Tui: joy
Success and happiness, but follow the course you know is right; period from August to October.

59. Huan: dispersing
Long-distance travel is favorable; rely on moral and spiritual values; June.

60. Chieh: limitations
Recognize your own failings; July.

61. Chung fu: inner truth
The path you are taking is the only one possible; have courage, be persistent; November.

62. Hsiao kuo: the powerful small
A time of small successes; do not undertake anything of great importance now; January.

63. Chi chi: after completion
Good fortune in the beginning but disorder at the end; October.

64. Wei chi: before completion
The present situation has more than halfway to go yet; keep plans flexible; November.

Tasseography
Divination from the tea leaves

The tea-leaf ritual in the West is not as old as many aspects of divining, dating only from the nineteenth century, when the custom of drinking tea was brought to the West by travelers from China and India. Today it satisfies our profound desire to read meaning into the world in which we live.

Because of the intimate situation in which the ritual was often performed—around the kitchen table—the interpretations are normally about love, family, home, and career, the matters which most affect us in such environments. In a reading the person who is being read for is the Querant.

Preparing the cup of tea

For the clearest symbols you should use tea with long stems and large leaves—China tea is best as it provides the biggest leaf patterns. Tea bags may be used only if you empty out the tea first. Take a large china teacup that you can dedicate strictly to tasseography. It will become your personal purveyor of wisdom. The tea must be brewed in a pot. Rinse the pot out first with boiling water to clear the debris and vibrations of the previous Querant, then bring the pot to the kettle—never carry the kettle to the pot.

The ritual of reading

Once the tea is poured, allow the Querant to drink the liquid to within ½ inch (12mm) of the bottom of the cup. This will ensure even distribution of the leaves later when the cup is inverted.

1. Having determined that the correct amount of liquid is left, the Querant should pick up the cup by the handle with their left hand and swirl it around three times clockwise, ensuring that the liquid reaches up to the rim of the cup and that the leaves are in a state of suspension in the remaining tea.

2. The Querant should then invert the cup onto the saucer either in a slow, deliberate movement or simply turned over very quickly. Leave the cup for at least seven seconds untouched to allow the liquid to drain away and the leaves to settle.

3. The reader now picks up the cup, turns it over, and holds it between both hands silently tuning in to the Querant's vibrations. Inside the cup lies the story of the future.

4. The Querant has now performed their part of the tasseography process and has relinquished the cup to the reader for the mysteries of the leaves to be divined. Now the reader's intuition and sensitivity are brought to bear to unlock the future. See pages 94–95 for interpretations.

Read from the left of the handle

Interpreting what you see

It is important that you do not hurry with the process of interpretation. Give it your fullest concentration so that your insight is engaged, enabling the pictures to become clear in your mind.

After you have identified the symbols, begin reading the cup from the left of the handle around to the middle of the opposite side, noticing the positioning of the symbols. Tradition says it spoils the luck the cup contains if you start from the right.

Some symbols will immediately spring out to you and are easily identified. Deal with these first. These may be the only ones necessary to give a comprehensive reading. Allow your instinct to form the shape for you—do not try too hard. Indeed, you may get only one symbol.

Events approaching

Events departing

Positions in the cup

When the teacup handle is held facing the reader the events depicted by the shapes on the left side of the handle signify approaching events, and the figures on the right departing. The nearer to the rim the patterns emerge, the closer in time they will happen; at the bottom of the cup lies the long-term prediction for the next 18 months.

Sample interpretations

A plane near the top of the cup predicts a journey taken in three months' time. Fortunate outcome.

The eye of opportunity. Because it is halfway down the cup be alert to fortunate prospects in the next six months.

A forked line near the rim of the cup suggests that a decision needs to be made quickly.

A butterfly represents good luck and happy times. Near the top of the cup it suggests a current winning streak.

A twig or branch implies fleeting new friendships and social activities.

Clouds halfway down the cup suggest doubt and lack of confidence will come in the next six months if a problem is left unsolved.

A clock at the bottom of the cup suggests that care needs to be taken with health. Overdoing things could lead to illness.

A chicken represents your abilities. Do not let anyone steal your ideas.

A ring symbol near the bottom of the cup indicates a relationship or friendship may end in the next six months.

Sortilege
The casting of lots

The word *sortilege*—fortune-telling by the casting or drawing of lots—comes from the Latin word *sors*, which means lots. The name *Sortilegus* is given to the person who is the reader or the diviner. The Greeks had their own name for the practice, cleromancy. The Delphic Oracle of Prophecy used to scatter beans to bring through extra knowledge. Orientals, Africans, and Asians also used objects for drawing lots.

Historically, virtually any object that was available was used to foretell the future. Classic modern-day examples are the lottery games played in many countries around the world: the "lots" are the numbered balls that fall at random. Sweepstakes, roulette, and bingo can also be included, in that they follow the principles of casting at random.

Allevromancy: the fortune cookie

At the end of a dinner, Chinese restaurants still offer a fortune cookie for good luck. This convention is a simple version of a method practiced in the early centuries by the use of paper and dough to construct a fortune sweetmeat. When a specific question needed to be answered, all the possible outcomes would be written on individual pieces of paper. Balls of sweet dough were prepared, and into each ball a hollow would be made, into which one of the pieces of paper was placed. The ball would then be closed, baked, and afterward placed into a dish. A cookie would be chosen at random and broken open. The answer to the question was then revealed by the slip of paper inside.

Instead of offering a cookie, just write your possible answers onto pieces of rice paper. Place them into cotton balls, and the

first one chosen will give the answer. Eating the rice-paper slip afterward will internally imbue a greater force of intention for luck to follow.

Belomancy: fortune-telling by arrows

An ancient divination art form practiced by the Babylonians, Arabs, and North American Indian tribes. Arrows were used for insight into the future because of the way they pierce the air—forward into the unknown. Each arrow was specifically marked, and either cast down onto the ground or drawn from a container.

The modern version of belomancy is the drawing of straws, where one is shorter than the rest, usually signifying bad luck. For a "yes" or "no" answer, put two straws of different lengths into a container on its side, with the two visible ends even. Ask your question, then draw out a straw. The long straw indicates "yes " and the shorter straw indicates "no."

Bibliomancy: opening a book at random

Since the human race could read, the written word has been a great source of enlightenment. It became only natural that books were included as tools for divination. The word bibliomancy comes from the Greek word *biblion*, meaning small book.

To find answers to your questions, close your eyes and, with the question firmly in your mind, open a chosen book and stop at a page at random. Use the forefinger of your left hand and let it be a pointer coming to rest on a word or sentence. This will give omens for good or bad luck.

Astragalomancy: the casting of bones

The casting of bones has been practiced since the beginning of humankind. Bones were thought to represent man's close connection with himself and nature. The bones were often respected for their healing powers and fertility, and were considered to bring good fortune (see also Dice on pages 100–101).

Casting bones

Oxtail bones can be used for this method.

1. Select the largest bone, which will represent strength and a promise of good fortune.

2. Select one to be the longest—this will indicate that the outcome will take a while to come to fruition.

3. Choose a bone that is damaged. This will show that care must be taken, as all is not well.

4. The fourth bone will be the smallest and will indicate that the outcome will not have much substance to it—it will be low-energy and lightweight.

5. Hold the bones in your right hand, ask your question, and scatter them before you. The bone that falls nearest to you gives the answer.

Pessomancy: divination by casting marked pebbles

Predicting the future using "talking stones" is another very ancient technique. You can mark even-sized pebbles with any symbol you like, or make your own code—such as a "fork," which would represent a crossroad ahead. You can also paint each stone a different color.

Stone Casting Method

A handful of colored or marked pebbles thrown to the winds can indicate future benefits and ills.

1. Select nine stones or pebbles that are the same size, round, and smooth.

2. Paint your stones with symbolic markings or colors.

3. Place the stones in your cupped hand. With your eyes closed, shake the stones, and concentrate on the area in which you need enlightenment.

4. Cast the stones down on an even surface, and open your eyes. The pebbles nearest you will represent happenings in the near future. The farther away they are, the longer the time until they occur.

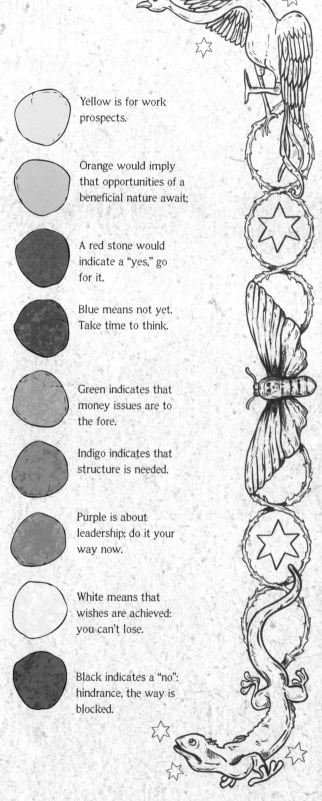

Yellow is for work prospects.

Orange would imply that opportunities of a beneficial nature await;

A red stone would indicate a "yes," go for it.

Blue means not yet. Take time to think.

Green indicates that money issues are to the fore.

Indigo indicates that structure is needed.

Purple is about leadership: do it your way now.

White means that wishes are achieved: you can't lose.

Black indicates a "no": hindrance, the way is blocked.

Dice Divination

Casting for answers

Divination by dice has its origins in astragalomancy, derived from the word astragalus, another word for ankle bone. Astragals were used in pairs, each one having four different faces upon which it could fall, which were assigned set values. Astragals in the shape of bones were even carved from semiprecious stones in Roman times. The values of these faces, plus two more, became the Roman six-sided die we are familiar with today.

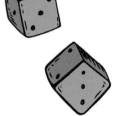

In ancient times, where the dice landed was very important. The dice were thrown onto a specific pattern related to nature, laid out on the ground. Crap tables today still adhere to a measured pattern, giving an indication of whether you are lucky or not, according to where the dice fall.

Divining by casting dice

The fall of the dice is determined by "meaningful coincidence." You should throw dice only on behalf of another—never for yourself. It may suit you best to work with the dice in complete silence. With practice, you will soon determine from your own experience what is appropriate for you. As a parlor game it is amusing for a few friends to compose lists of questions and answers for themselves, or you can use dice for more serious divination.

The keys for success

To begin, draw a circle about the diameter of two spread hands. The circle symbolizes an all-encompassing area. It will allow the dice and the elements to focus on the specific question asked. It is absolutely paramount that only one question be asked at a time for each throw of the dice. The dice cannot answer several questions at once.

Counting the dice

If both dice land in the circle, add up the two numbers revealed. If one die falls outside, do not count it. If both dice fall outside, throw again.

1. Think of the question, and throw the dice into the circle.

2. Add up the numbers revealed and consult the list of answers below.

3. If one die falls outside the circle, do not count it.

4. If both dice come to rest outside, throw them again.

5. If both dice come to rest outside again, it is not a favorable time for an answer to your question. Do not throw them a third time.

6. Use the list of answers below, or construct your own.

1	=	Yes
2	=	No
3	=	Take care
4	=	Be wise
5	=	Excellent luck
6	=	Of course
7	=	Have faith
8	=	Patience
9	=	Certainly
10	=	Doubtful
11	=	Nonsense
12	=	A risk

Chapter 5

Summoning the Waking Vision

The techniques in this chapter require the input of the intellect, rather than the purely intuitive. These techniques were usually the province of the initiates, who developed a fine and sophisticated balance of intellect and intuition. Three specific skills have been chosen to allow your perception and insight to be trained and developed.

Start with numerology and cartomancy in order to develop your skills in combining both intellect and intuition. Once these skills are developed you will be ready to turn to the Tarot. Most fortune-tellers suggest using ordinary playing cards before moving on to the complex symbolic richness of the Tarot. The oldest surviving complete Tarot decks date from around the middle of the fifteenth century. How much earlier the Tarot itself dates from is hotly debated: suggestions include the initiate-rulers of long lost Atlantis, the priest-magicians of ancient Egypt, and a college of wise men who flourished in the North African city of Fez. Wherever it originated, it contains powerful and universal images.

While both numerology and cartomancy can be used for serious readings or simple party tricks, the Tarot is another matter altogether. Its understanding and proper use involves extended study, and the experienced Tarot reader will eventually read on as many as eight different levels for any single card. Beyond the simple introduction to the cards in this book, the serious student will need to embark upon further study, and training with an experienced reader may be required. What is possible here is an introduction to the cards, and a simple familiarization process. The Tarot should always be treated with respect, because embodied within the deck is the whole of Earth's history.

Numerology

Your future in figures

Most of us have heard such expressions as "he thought his number was up" or "my lucky number had come up." These casually used phrases reflect an ancient belief that from any individual's name it is possible to derive a number (or numbers) that is of great significance in that person's life, and provides a key to the secrets of his or her character and destiny.

There are many numerology systems, but the actual meanings of the numbers, drawn largely from the Kabbala and astrology, are generally agreed upon. You will find that the interpretations of these meanings can differ considerably among numerologists. The numbers are derived by giving a number equivalent to each letter of the alphabet, usually based on the following simple table:

1	2	3	4	5	6	7	8	9
a	b	c	d	e	f	g	h	i
j	k	l	m	n	o	p	q	r
s	t	u	v	w	x	y	z	

The meanings of the numbers

There are several basic numbers that are derived by numerologists. In advanced numerology there are other numbers that can be obtained, but they are beyond the scope of this book; the numbers you can easily derive for yourself will give you highly valuable insights.

There are four numbers that reflect the various aspects of your life:

Your key number The whole person.
Your personality number Outward impressions.
Your destiny number Life's lessons.
Your heart number The inner personality; the basic fabric of your being.

The destiny and heart numbers are the most reflective of the framework within which your life's lessons are structured.

Finding your destiny number

Your destiny number is calculated from your date of birth. It is the one unchangeable number in your life: you can change your name, from which other numbers are calculated, but not your birth. To calculate your destiny number, write down your date of birth in numerical form, and add up the numbers, ignoring the zeros. Then add up the numbers in this result to get your destiny number. Say you were born on October 22nd, 1944. Write:

$$1 + 2 + 2 + 1 + 9 + 4 + 4 = 23$$
$$2 + 3 = 5$$

So, your destiny number is 5. It shows the lessons that you are working through in this lifetime (see pages 108–109 for interpretations).

Finding your heart number

The real, inner you is revealed through your heart number. Your heart number is calculated from the vowels in your name, using the table, opposite. If your name is John Smith, the vowel equivalents are:

There are only two vowels, giving you a total of 6 + 9 = 15; 1 + 5 = 6. Therefore, your heart number is 6 (see pages 108–109 for interpretations).

```
    6           9
 JOHN    SMITH
```

Interpreting your numbers

Once you have found your destiny and heart numbers, you will find in the interpretations on the right an understanding relating to each of those numbers. You discover the key words for destiny number five are restless, traveler, intelligent, communicator, and self-indulgent; and for the heart number six they are kind-hearted, loving, considerate, caring, home-loving, creative, artistic, complacent, self-satisfied, conceited. From this is indicated that you are a person of wide-ranging talents and abilities, that will all add up to a very attractive personality when fully realized. But, care will have to be taken not to let those qualities lead you into self-satisfaction, self-indulgence, and self-centeredness.

For a person with this combination of positive and negative traits, it will be necessary to cultivate an unusually strong character. You could also conclude that life will throw you a great many challenges to test that strength of character. Having been gifted with so many opportunities, you must be careful to make the most of them and not let them slip away.

Number interpretations

One

Destiny
The pioneer; independent; inventive; ambitious; obstinate; bossy; overly single-minded.

Heart
Ambitious; energetic; confident; innovative; feelings of superiority.

Two

Destiny
Passive; supportive; considerate; harmonious; moody; secretive.

Heart
Sensitive; sympathetic; oversensitive; diffident; supportive partner; deceitful.

Seven

Destiny
Psychic; intuitive; sensitive; imaginative; withdrawn; remote.

Heart
Misunderstood; high ideals; single-minded; withdrawn; otherworldly.

Eight

Destiny
Hard-working; achiever; status-seeking.

Heart
Ambitious; inner-driven; materialistic; loyal; dependable; stand-offish; sarcastic; rude.

Three

Destiny
Happy relationships; warm; cheerful; optimistic; self-display.

Heart
Cheerful; optimistic; amusing; likeable; cheap popularity.

Four

Destiny
Discipline; willpower; organizational skills; practical; narrow-minded; zealous; apathetic.

Heart
Shy; hardworking; reliable; depressed; violent mood swings.

Five

Destiny
Restless; traveler; intelligent; communicator; self-indulgent.

Heart
Restless; lively; charming; versatile; extreme eccentricity.

Six

Destiny
Homemaker; reliable; possessive; insular.

Heart
Kind-hearted; loving; considerate; homeloving; creative; artistic; complacent; self-satisfied; conceited.

Nine

Destiny
Visionary; enthusiastic; competitive; despondent; inconsiderate; wayward; impractical.

Heart
Curious; analytical; romantic; loving; helpful; nosy; dominating.

Eleven and twenty-two are the only double-figure numbers regarded as important in the numerological analysis of personal names.

Eleven

Destiny
Resolute; successful; popular; respected; exploitative; impractical.

Heart
Idealistic; world-changer; unstoppable; uncaring; single-minded.

Twenty-two

Destiny
Capable; industrious; practical; brilliant; complacent.

Heart
Inner potential; humanitarian; overpowering; moral perversion.

Cartomancy
Divination by playing cards

There is a certain arbitrary nature to the assigned meanings of the ordinary cards, but the principle of "meaningful coincidence" works just as well as with the Tarot deck—the shuffle of the deck adapts itself to the meanings that are attributed to the cards and the pattern in which they are going to fall. The meanings listed below are those shown to work for many fortune-tellers.

Instructions for a reading

The cards can point to many things in your life: relationships; your past, present, and future; your weaknesses; your strengths and hidden abilities; and much more.

1. Focus on the question to be answered.

2. Shuffle the cards as normal.

3. Cut and reshuffle the cards twice more.

4. Draw the cards from the top of the deck, and place them as indicated by the layout. Refer to the tables below and opposite to interpret the cards.

Card 1   Card 2   Card 3

Aspects of your question

Theme	Card 1	Card 2	Card 3
Past, present, future	Past	Present	Future
Current situation	Love Life	Health	Career
Life's strengths	Creativity	Talents	Hidden abilities
Life's weaknesses	Prejudice	Blindness	Unseen failing
Relationships	Family	Friends	Personal
What to do next	Immediate	Soon	Later
What are my choices?	Best	Moderate	Worst

Meanings of the cards

Hearts ♥	Clubs ♣	Spades ♠	Diamonds ♦	
Your physical base: home. Your emotional base: love, friendship, and affection.	Wealth; prosperity; events leading to material success.	Positive new adventures.	Extraordinary but unpredictable good luck; a good beginning.	Ace
Partnership, usually between lovers, close friends, or relations.	Material losses; business disputes; disagreements over money.	Forward movement; new starts.	Prudent action brings increased prosperity.	Two
Friendship, sociability, and enjoyable encounters.	Sluggishness, inertia; delays in financial matters; unwelcome intervention.	Plans and ideas solidified.	The cooperation of those close brings good luck.	Three
Enduring emotional relationships.	Prosperity; financial success; good luck	Foresight brings luck and prosperity.	Solid advancement and good fortune.	Four
Uncertain love; emotional disturbance.	Disharmony; quarrels; obstacles; financial and property disputes.	Turmoil; disputes; disorder; partings.	Differences of opinion bring conflict.	Five
Solid affection; offers of love; welcome invitations.	Unusually good luck; prosperity; luck in financial matters.	It is time to move on, physically or mentally.	Lasting happiness in all things.	Six
Fulfilling sexual relationships; love triumphant.	Wasted money; financial losses; money worries; foolish speculation.	Quarrels and breakups with partners; accidents.	Strong bonds form in a passionate relationship.	Seven
Romantic communications; tranquil love.	Documents relating to business or money; money from investment.	Journeys; surprises; arrivals; departures; positive communications	Excitement and adventure.	Eight
Wishes fulfilled; fertility.	Money matters relating to relationships; a comfortable financial situation.	Distressing but impermanent family disputes.	A joyful union; birth; positive change for the better.	Nine
Material happiness; financial prosperity.	Material success.	Things are not as good as they seem; disappointments.	Tranquility returns; money arrives—finally.	Ten
Impulsive affection; an admirer.	A young person, not always trustworthy, connected to money.	A young man or woman full of energy and ideas.	An aggressive young person, but not lacking in positive traits.	Jack
Strong emotions emanate from a mature woman.	A sound, well-grounded, mature woman.	A lively and active mature woman.	An assertive, mature woman.	Queen
An affectionate man of any age, seeking love.	A reliable, mature man; the inquirer's employer.	A mature man full of the vigors of life.	A tireless, mature man.	King

The Tarot

Divining with Tarot cards

An ordinary deck of cards is made up of four suits, each consisting of ten pip cards, from ace to ten, and three court cards, King, Queen, and Knave (or Jack), as well as one or two Jokers, or Fools. The standard Tarot deck is similarly structured, but there are also 21 other cards known as trumps or the Major Arcana, usually numbered in Roman numerals. The joker is numberless or numbered 0.

While the Tarot is mainly used for fortune-telling, many people today also use these cards for self-exploration and personal growth, and there is a game of Tarot (or tarok) still played in central Europe. Many of the earliest known decks were designed by artists, including the most famous artist of Reformation Germany, Albrecht Dürer.

Highly respected
Within the cornucopia of fortune-telling methods available to the seeker, the Tarot is, for professional seers, among the most respected.

Shuffling the cards

The first step in reading the cards is always to shuffle them in the correct manner as described below. The reason is that an ordinary playing card is always the right side up. When Tarot cards are used for divination, their meanings are not the same when they are reversed— upside down. You should shuffle your Tarot cards in this way each time you use them. The inquirer should focus on their specific question, and then:

1. Cut the deck into two roughly equal parts.

2. Turn one half of the deck upside down and put it on top of the other half.

3. Shuffle the cards thoroughly.

4. Repeat steps 1–3 twice.

5. Draw the topmost card, turning it over clockwise from left to right.

Reading the Tarot

The pattern in which cards are laid out as they are chosen is called a spread. There are several standard spreads, but simple spreads involving only a few cards are recommended at the beginning in order to gain proficiency, to start getting a feel for the cards, and to learn the technique of combining the meanings of cards into a coherent whole.

First-level reading

For the purpose of familiarizing yourself with the deck, work with a single card to receive indications of the answer to the inquirer's question. It is to be emphasized that this is not a "reading" as such, but a way of familiarizing yourself with the cards.

The standard Tarot deck

There are other Tarot decks in addition to the standard, but as an introduction we will stay with the standard one. Where other decks use different terms for either the suits or the individual cards, the most common of those appear in parentheses.

The divinatory meanings of the Tarot cards

There are other and more detailed meanings to each of the cards, but here are listed the key words for each relating specifically to divination.

Wands (Batons or Staves)

Ace
Beginnings; renewal; birth; activity; energy; success; achievement.
Reversed Failure; overreaching; inadequate effort.

Two
Power; wealth; good fortune.
Reversed The unexpected; suffering.

Three
Material success.
Reversed Difficulties to overcome; or failure results from excessive ambition.

Four
Successful conclusions; contented home life; happy retirement.
Reversed The same, but more so.

Five
Arguments; trials; struggle; success after struggle.
Reversed Disputes and quarrels turned to advantage.

Six
Success through hard work.
Reversed Disloyalty; beware of treachery.

Seven
A serious threat to self-reliance and inner strength.
Reversed Dangerous indecision.

Eight
Everything rushes toward a conclusion; domestic disagreements; infatuation.
Reversed Disputes and jealousy at home; a theft; a swindle.

Nine
Strength, resistance, persistence. Objectives and desires achieved; recovery from illness.
Reversed Irritating delays; obstacles prevent satisfactory conclusions.

Ten
Misuse of energy; materialism; selfishness; injustice; inadequate satisfaction from success.
Reversed Material losses, perhaps the result of deceit.

Page
A likeable stranger comes into the inquirer's life; for a female inquirer, this could be a faithful lover.
Reversed The receipt of unreliable information concerning matters indicated by the cards to the left and right of it in a more detailed spread.

Swords

Knight
A man who has bouts of furious energy, but lacks staying power; hasty decisions and actions.
Reversed A narrow-minded/cruel person; rows; disruptions.

Queen
A woman of charm with a dislike of opposition, who deals calmly with practical matters; financial success.
Reversed A virtuous woman who takes offense to small matters and is likely to act on impulse.

King
An honest, generous man with all the old-fashioned virtues. When not symbolizing a person: a fortunate love partnership or an inheritance.
Reversed An intolerant, inflexible, and ungenerous man.

Ace
Male sexuality; the beginning of a powerful relationship; forces outside the inquirer's control; success in spite of all obstacles, or utter failure.
Reversed The same, but stronger and usually more malefic.

Two
Balanced forces; harmony reigns; an end to pain, physical or emotional; an end to disagreements or quarrels.
Reversed Trouble and treachery.

Three
Disruption, dis-equilibriums, and separation—sometimes temporary.
Reversed Confusion, strife, and trouble.

Four
Conflict ends; harmony is restored; tensions ease.
Reversed Be cautious; sometimes foretells a legacy.

Five:
Failure, defeat, anxiety, and depression; a trouble-maker is working against the interests of the inquirer.

Reversed The same, but maybe even more so.

Six
Success through effort; an improving situation; a happy journey.
Reversed Surprises in the inquirer's emotional life.

Seven
A fluid situation or an unreliable person; show persistence and do not make hasty compromises.
Reversed Good advice arrives; prudence on the part of the inquirer.

Eight
A crisis imposing restraints and limitations. Examine all aspects before entering into binding agreements.
Reversed An unforeseen frustration or an unpleasant surprise

Nine
Self-sacrifice; personal suffering voluntarily undertaken; misfortune; desolation.
Reversed An unreliable person; justified suspicion; onset of loneliness.

Ten

Hopes destroyed and/or grief; can indicate that it is the opponents and rivals of the inquirer who will come to grief; can also indicate loss of a set of false beliefs. **Reversed** Temporary advantages; failure follows success.

Page

Indicates a subtle-minded young person who is conscious of the feeling of others, graceful, and well-coordinated. **Reversed** A devious, frivolous young person; or unexpected news or a surprising turn of events.

Knight

A forceful man who is a good friend, but a dangerous opponent; also, personal enmity becomes significant in the matter the inquiry is about. **Reversed** For a male inquirer, a dominating but very foolish person who is constantly changing; for a female inquirer, a rival who will be overcome.

Queen

Can indicate either any mature woman or general unhappiness, particularly that caused by loneliness. **Reversed** Attitudes of prudishness; or a deceitful and malicious woman.

King

A man who occupies a position of some responsibility such as a physician or an official. He may make foolish decisions despite his high opinion of himself. **Reversed** A selfish, calculating, untrustworthy man, especially in legal matters.

Cups (Chalices)

Ace

Very lucky; abundance; fertility; fruitful enterprises; a declaration of love. **Reversed** Unfaithfulness; unwelcome or unhappy endings.

Two

Marriage; deep love; sympathetic understanding; holidays. **Reversed** Extravagance; self-indulgence; break-ups.

Three

Good fortune; abundance; success; favorable conclusions. **Reversed** Excessive pleasure; rapid and fortunate endings.

Four

Stagnation and boredom in an otherwise happy situation; good and bad fortune alternate. **Reversed** Great and novel change.

Five

Friendship and love bring disappointment; tears follow laughter; unexpected reactions. **Reversed** Plans go awry; sudden and unexpected comings and goings.

Six
Looking backward and nostalgia; or its opposite—a future situation.
Reversed Something about to happen—the next card dealt indicates what.

Seven
A misused talent; illusion and false glamour; illusionary success.
Reversed A time of plans, undertakings, and wishes.

Eight
Unjustified dissatisfaction with past achievements; a new path in life.
Reversed General happiness.

Nine
Good luck with finance and possessions; fulfillment; recovery from illness.
Reversed Mistakes and miscalculations.

Ten
Physical well-being; spiritual advancement; material and intellectual success.
Reversed Quarrels; disputes; tread carefully.

Page
Thinking in depth about a situation; good or bad news.
Reversed Infidelity; deception; a lying deceiver.

Knight
Messages or propositions arrive, determined by the cards dealt immediately before or after.
Reversed Deception; fraud; an unreliable person.

Queen
A flirtatious or teasing woman; a shallow woman.
Reversed Cunning; malice; cattiness; an evil woman.

King
A hostile superior; a man in a position of responsibility, who is helpful only to those who are useful to him.
Reversed Dishonesty; deceit; an evil and dishonest man.

Pentacles (Coins or Disks)

Ace
Extreme good fortune concerning money, property, and material possessions; prosperity; security; a successful career.
Reversed The negative side of good fortune; greed; ruthlessness; overvalue of worldly possessions.

Two
Material opposites; alternating good and bad fortune; successful and unsuccessful projects; mood swings from high to low.
Reversed Things are the opposite of what they seem.

Three
An improved situation; new projects favored; imminent promotion.
Reversed The opposite, but less emphatic.

Four
Material success; achievement; financial security.
Reversed Delay; uncertainty; a fluid situation.

Five

Material, career, and financial concerns; there may be a temporary loss of money, job, or home.
Reversed Danger of heavy financial losses through extravagance, gambling, or unwise speculation.

Six

Prosperity as a result of help from others.
Reversed Financial reverses resulting from envy and greed.

Seven

Something wrong financially.
Reversed The same, but with more disappointment and worry.

Eight:

Small improvements; too much attention to matters of minor importance.
Reversed Danger from dishonest financial dealings—may even be the inquirer's.

Nine

Material good fortune; a large inheritance; a large increase in income.
Reversed Material loss results from the deceit of others.

Ten

Great material success after years of effort.
Reversed Material or financial losses from theft or dishonesty.

Page

Good management and prudence; a hard-working, methodical person who can be trusted with money.
Reversed An extravagant or careless person in money matters; imminent bad news about finances.

Knight

A dull, but hard-working and conscientious man; a boring but necessary task to complete.
Reversed A lazy, careless person; problems caused by laziness or carelessness.

Queen

Generosity; warm sincerity; a down-to-earth woman.
Reversed An unreliable woman; unreliability; unpredictability.

King

Quiet energy; steadfastness; implacability; a devoted friend or lover, although seldom demonstrative; a practical man in late middle or old age.
Reversed A cruel and corrupt man.

Trumps (the Major Arcana)

The Tarot trumps depict a person's journey through life and their spiritual growth. They represent both major and minor life events, and add important details that contribute to a comprehensive picture within whichever reading the inquirer undertakes.

The success of a reading can depend on a number of elements, including the reader's skill in interpreting the cards, and whether the reader and the inquirer are psychically compatible.

0 The Joker
(The Fool/Jester)
Foolishness; eccentricity; the bizarre; unexpected/surprising events; a new beginning or change of direction.
Reversed Procrastination—putting things off until tomorrow. Carelessness, laziness, and an inability or unwillingness to make decisions.

I The Magician
(The Juggler)
Favors everyday risks; initiative; skills; general adaptability; something or somebody new.
Reversed Uncertainty; deception; confusion; an individual who aims to deceive.

II The High Priestess
(The Popess/Pope Joan)
Secrets; the hidden intuition; change.
Reversed Perilous sexual passion.

III The Empress
Happiness; good fortune; pleasurable experiences.
Reversed Fruitless effort; conflict; disagreements; an unproductive person.

IV The Emperor
Ambition; success; creativity.
Reversed Obstruction; limitation; lack of progress; over-confidence.

V The High Priest (The Pope/The Hierophant)
Mystical and esoteric matters; help comes from a friend; a compatible marriage partner.
Reversed Deceit; bad advice; disloyalty.

VI The Lovers (Vice and Virtue/The Two Paths)
Love; sexual attraction; a choice to be made.
Reversed Endings, separations, and partings.

VII The Chariot
(The Sphinxes)
Overcoming all difficulties; success; travel; unexpected change.
Reversed Bad news or bad luck.

VIII Justice
The inquirer is put to the test; a time for decisions.
Reversed Injustice; things go wrong.

VIIII The Hermit (The Hunchback/The Old Man)
Wise counsel; prudence; tact; an elderly person.
Reversed Inactivity; delay; secrecy; indecisiveness.

X The Wheel Of Fortune
Good luck; financial success; favorable changes.
Reversed Unfavorable changes and happenings.

XI Strength (Force)
Inner strength; fortitude; self-discipline; a favorable female influence.
Reversed The opposite.

XII The Hanged Man
Odd behavior; setbacks;
sacrifice.
Reversed Pain; suffering;
uncaring people.

XIII Death
Loss; disappointment;
failure; partings,
loss of help.
Reversed Long life;
rebirth; regeneration;
problems resolved; a
desired transformation.

XIIII Temperance
(Intemperance)
Successful partnerships;
a happy outcome; good
health; recovery from
illness.
Reversed Disputes;
disagreements; difficult
situation.

XV The Devil
Temptation; obsessive
physical sexuality;
obsessions about money
and possessions.
Reversed Foolishness;
miserliness; malice; an
unfortunate happening.

XVI The Tower (The
Blasted Tower/
The House of God):
War; conflict; accidents;
quarrels; material losses.
Reversed The same, but
worse.

XVII The Star
Unexpected assistance
from a powerful person;
good luck; a very fortunate
happening.
Reversed The opposite.

XVIII The Moon
Adventures; risk; major
changes; uncertain motives
of others.
Reversed Small changes.

XVIIII The Sun
Prosperity; success; joy
and fulfillment.
Reversed The same but
not as strong.

XX The Last Judgment
Fresh starts; old problems
solved; important
decisions; reunions.
Reversed Muddle; delay;
indecision; confusion;
inconclusive solutions.

XXI The World
(The Universe/The System)
Certain success after
long effort; travel or
immigration; welcome
change.
Reversed Failure;
stagnation; boredom;
inadequate rewards.

Glossary

Many terms are defined in this book, some in more detail than others. In this glossary, further definition is provided.

Augurist From the word augur, a Roman religious official who foretold the future based on such omens as the movements of birds and the actions of animals.

Augury The act of divining by omens, especially omens presented by the daily activities of nature.

Cartomancy A term applied to divination by means of an ordinary deck of playing cards and other decks of cards that have been specifically created for prediction purposes. This term is not usually applied to divination through the use of the Tarot.

Clairvoyance Literally "clear seeing," the ability to receive information from unseen forces or through visions, often involving future events.

Divination The action of acquiring insight into the unknown through the use of powers, activities, objects, and abilities that reflect that which is beyond the normal senses.

Dowsing A term meaning divining for water or minerals through the use of a forked stick. The term is more generally applied to the use of the pendulum to divine information about the future, the unseen, or the unknown.

Element Refers to that which is a primal force of nature: earth; air; fire; water.

Inquirer The person who is making a query of the gods or the diviner.

Lot Each of a set of objects used to divine; as in "the casting of lots." A lot can be any object that is used in this way, such as bones, stones, and sticks.

Medium Term used for the person conducting or giving a psychic reading. This person becomes the mediator between heaven and earth.

Omen A warning of good or evil to come, reflected in objects, occurrences, or prophecy.

Oracle In ancient times it referred to the place where prophecy was offered. It also refers to the person through whom prophecy occurs—usually a woman.

Psychic As a noun, the receiver of information and insights without logical reason; as an adjective, having these qualities.

Querant Based on the word "query"; the person for whom information is being sought in the act of divination, or for whom the future is being foretold; also known as the "sitter."

Reader The person who is performing the act of divination, especially when it involves objects being "read," such as cards, colors, runes, and the *I Ching*.

Reading Another term for the act of divining, in which the "reader" obtains an answer to a question or questions posed by the querant.

Runes An ancient Teutonic alphabet used by Scandinavians and Anglo-Saxons from the second to the tenth centuries, the letters of which were derived by modifying Greek or Roman letters; each of these letters was in itself believed to embody certain specific magical forces.

Seer A person who possesses the ability to foretell future events through insight or visions, or by acts of divination.

Spread Any definite arrangement of cards for a specific divinatory purpose. There are a number of established spreads for specific types of readings.

Index

Credits

Quarto would like to thank and acknowledge the following for supplying pictures reproduced in this book:

p.37: Elsa Godfrey

p.39: jara77/Shutterstock.com

p.58 symbols: MysticalLink/Shutterstock.com

p.79: AKaiser/Shutterstock.com

p.112: Francesco Abrignani/Shutterstock.com.